GROWING OLD
IN THE
COUNTRY
OF
THE YOUNG

GROWING OLD IN THE COUNTRY OF THE YOUNG

United States Senator
CHARLES H. PERCY

McGraw-Hill Book Company

New York   St. Louis   San Francisco   Düsseldorf
Mexico   Sydney   Toronto

Book Design, Robert L. Mitchell

23456789 BPBP 798765

Library of Congress Cataloging in Publication Data

Percy, Charles H   1919–
    Growing old in the country of the young.

    1. Aged—United States. I. Title.
HV1461.P47   362.6'0973   74-13940
ISBN 0-07-049315-4

To my mother,
Elisabeth Harting Percy,
the youngest of us all.

Preface

In a way, we all are experts on the old, or at least we should be. Nearly all of us have elderly relatives, elderly friends; more often than not, their lives are visibly hard. In my own case, the lives of my parents long ago opened my eyes to both the problems and the potential of growing old in the country of the young. My father's difficulty in finding work during the early '30s ("Sorry, we're looking for someone younger") taught me a harsh lesson about age-discrimination—discrimination which is every bit as real today as it was then.

At the age of eighty-two, my mother is still showing me that one's later years can be a joyous culmination of all that has come before. Fortunate in that she enjoys good health and has an adequate income, she remains a vigorous, vibrant, loving woman. Devoted to her family, friends, church and community (among other things, she plays first violin in the Evanston Symphony Orchestra), she celebrates life and so enhances it.

If my "expertise" in this field is somewhat greater than average, it is because my much-maligned profession—politics—has brought me into fairly close contact with thousands of elderly Americans. As a United States Senator from Illinois, my constituency includes 11 million people, more than a million of whom are over sixty-five. It is part of my job to know their problems and concerns.

As a member of the Senate's Special Committee on Aging and as the senior Republican on the Select Committee on Nutrition and Human Needs, I have had an unusual opportunity to study and frequently to witness firsthand the trials of our older citizens. It has been an unsettling education.

In the pages to follow, we have concentrated on those aspects of old age in America which seem at once most severe and pervasive: inadequacies in income, housing, nutrition, medical and institutional "care," and, perhaps most poignant of all, the isolation of our elders. At the same time, we have tried to suggest what can be done to uplift the living conditions of older people. On a limited scale, as you will see, some of it is being done already. Generally, however, a much broader national commitment will be required if we are to fully restore dignity and purpose to the lives of elderly Americans; we have proposed specific ways that commitment could be shaped.

In the "Action Guide" starting on page 119, we have assembled information, often state by state, which can lead interested readers to a wide variety of existing services for the elderly.

In no sense is this book a scientific study. Instead, I think of it as an impressionistic survey; by focusing on the lives of a few individuals, we have tried to illuminate the lives of many. (To protect the privacy of these individuals, we often have used pseudonyms.)

I would hope that for those who read it, this book will be just a beginning toward a more active personal and civic interest in the problems of the elderly. It is intended, really, to be a consciousness-raising book; if it succeeds in even modestly heightening a collective awareness of what it is like to grow old in America, it will have served its purpose.

A final word on how the book was written:

I have used the word "we" in describing the intent of this volume, because *Growing Old in the Country of the Young* is very much a cooperative effort.

I'm not sure I have the talent, and I know I don't have the time, to write a book completely on my own. My contribution to this one consisted of the original idea; hundreds of hours of field research in nursing homes, housing projects, senior centers, hospitals and in Senate investigative hearings; more hours spent tape-recording my experiences and ideas on the subject; and a fair share of reorganizing and rewriting. Since the book is published under my name, and since I had the final say on every aspect of it, I take full responsibility for its flaws. Any credit, however, is truly shared by many.

Much of the credit for the editorial focus must go to writer Charles Mangel, who helped me define problems and solutions. Charlie's humanity is continually reflected in his work. His skill and sensitivity were indispensable to this book.

In addition to Mr. Mangel and our forbearing editor, Fred Hills, a number of other people have made essential contributions to this effort.

Vernon Goetcheus, Minority Counsel on the Senate Select Committee on Nutrition and Human Needs, and Constance Beaumont, a former member of my staff who now serves as Director of Governmental Affairs, American Association of Homes for the Aging, have been of great help in developing programs to benefit the elderly. Julia Bloch, John Childers, Tom Flaherty, and Tom Daffron brought their expertise and customary professionalism to the project.

The American Association of Retired Persons– National Retired Teachers' Association, the National Council of Senior Citizens, and the National Council on the Aging has each provided me with expert technical assistance and counsel; their continuing work in behalf of elderly Americans is a national resource. Jack Ossofsky, Rebecca Eckstein and Marjorie A. Collins of NCOA were particularly helpful.

William Recktenwald, chief investigator of Illinois' Better Government Association, has kindly accompanied me through the years on my periodic visits to nursing homes, and has done much to broaden my understanding of that entire industry.

Jeanne Paul spent long hours researching the Action Resource Guide, with volunteer assistance from Carol Simmons and Rob Tunnicliff. Extensive revisions were made by Steve Schreiber, who has been helpful in a variety of ways. Without the efforts of all of them the Guide would have been impossible.

Virginia Bottoms, Donna Harper, Bonita Herby, Alexis McMillan, Lucille Paaske, Carol Phillips, Alison Rosenberg and, particularly, Beki Morris all helped to type and proof the manuscript.

John Walker, whose editorial support was especially helpful, made a major contribution to these pages.

And, finally, the overall assistance of my longtime friend and adviser, Calvin Fentress, was invaluable.

My family shares my interest in America's most neglected minority. My mother, my wife Loraine, Sharon and Jay, Roger and Penny, Gail and Mark, my sister Doris Strauss and my brother Howard—between them, they have visited scores of nursing homes and housing projects for the elderly; their concern and observations have contributed much to my own awareness of the problems at hand.

To them, and to all others who helped along the way, many, many thanks. And to the older Americans whose lives fill this book, and who cooperated so graciously in its preparation, I extend both my thanks and my respectful admiration for their courage and their spirit.

C.H.P.
Washington, D.C.
August 1974

Table of Contents

ACTION RESOURCE GUIDE

1.

IN THE COUNTRY OF THE YOUNG

To Mrs. Jean Rosenstein of Los Angeles, to be old means being "so lonely I could die." Mrs. Rosenstein, an elderly widow who lives in a cramped, $60-a-month apartment near a freeway, wrote a letter to the *Los Angeles Times:*

"I see no human beings. My phone never rings. I feel sure the world has ended. I'm the only one on earth. How else can I feel? All alone. The people here won't talk to you. They say, 'Pay your rent and go back to your room.' I'm so lonely, very, very much. I don't know what to do. . . ."

Mrs. Rosenstein enclosed $1 and six stamps with her letter. "Will someone please call me?" she asked. The dollar was to pay for the call; the stamps were to be used if anyone would write to her. As the

Times pointed out, in that city of nearly 3 million people, Jean Rosenstein, age eighty-four, had no one.

In some primitive societies, the aged, seen as an economic burden, are killed. With too many of our own elderly, we achieve the same effect more subtly.

We value productivity. If someone is not "productive" (is that word to be measured only in terms of Gross National Product?), he or she has little value. "The minute we meet someone, we ask, 'What do you do?' " says Dr. Jack Weinberg, director of the Illinois State Psychiatric Institute. "That places the person within a framework we can understand and cope with. But if you meet a man and ask him what he does and he says, 'Nothing,' you're stymied, as if he seems *to be* nothing." Too often, that is precisely our attitude toward the aged in America.

"To our nation's shame, many are hidden in the slums of urban centers, barely surviving," reports one observer. "Eventually they face placement in a substandard nursing home or a state mental hospital. Or they die alone, unnoticed."

In Miami not long ago, two elderly men—critically ill, homeless, penniless—were put into wheelchairs to sit in a jammed aisle of a hospital until nursing home space could be found for them. Both men died in those chairs and it was hours before anyone even noticed they were dead. One man had been sitting in his chair for three days and the other man for two.

As the hospital told of the deaths of these men, ten more just like them were still sitting in that aisle.

Indifference towards older citizens pervades our

national laws. Jacqueline Hosanna, sixty-seven, and Samuel Pell, seventy, of Albuquerque, New Mexico, both lost their spouses to serious illness a number of years ago. Candidly, they admit they live together. "We'd like to get married," Mrs. Hosanna says, "but our government penalizes us if we do. I'm now getting 85 percent of my late husband's Social Security check. If I remarry, I'll receive only half of Mr. Pell's. And we can't afford that loss." Rather than be concerned about two basic human needs—companionship and love—we force many of our elderly to live a lie.

If they are timid, they turn away from this closeness in their last years. "I'm writing to ask a favor," a recent letter to me began. "I am sixty-five years old. My friend is, too. We want to get married. I can't afford to give up my income, $393.60 a month. This Social Security was rightfully earned by my deceased husband. Why should I have to forsake this income if I get married? Living alone is miserable. Can't you do something?"

At a time in their lives when they need more rather than fewer services, older people suffer drastic drops in income. Just when they discover that their bodies are less nimble, they find that transportation costs are rising—if the service has not disappeared altogether. When they find it necessary to buy more medication and to visit doctors more frequently, they see medical costs climb out of reach.

And, finally, at an age when, because of decreased mobility, inadequate income and declining health, they feel the greatest need to live in comfortable, familiar surroundings, close to the people they know and love—something that could be made possible if the community provided the barest of home services—older Americans frequently are forced to give up their homes or are shunted off to institutions.

"We seem to believe that every 'problem' has some sort of institutional solution," wrote nurse Sharon Curtin in *Nobody Ever Died of Old Age.* "Now that we are beginning to realize that the aged in our society are a 'problem,' we respond by creating new institutions. New nursing homes and new retirement centers are all places where the aged are segregated from the rest of the community and, thus, invisible. It is a ridiculous response to the needs of the elderly. They need more, not less, involvement with the community."

It's little wonder that people over sixty-five make up almost 30 percent of the residents of public mental hospitals and constitute almost 20 percent of all first admissions. "Much of their mental impairment springs from the reduction of opportunities for human contact," says The President's Task Force on the Mentally Handicapped. "Boredom is frequently a contributory factor." The Committee on Aging of the American Medical Association studied "aging" for fifteen years and reported, "There is no mental condition that results from the passage of time."

Too many people believe too many false things about the elderly. "As far as we know, nothing says biologically that at age sixty-five somebody should not be as active as he was at fifty-five," says Dr. Carl Eisdorfer of the University of Washington Medical School, Seattle.

There are a number of myths we clutch as truths:

Most of the aged are disabled.

Eighty-nine percent of all men and women over sixty-five live in the community and are totally self-sufficient. Only 7 percent are confined to their beds or to their homes. Just 4 percent live in institutions.

Most of the elderly suffer from serious mental deterioration and senility.

Intelligence, as measured in tests of comprehension and knowledge, shows little or no decline for the average elderly person. "Mental deterioration rarely occurs among normal older people before the eighties," says Dr. Robert E. Rothenberg. Evidence indicates the ability to think and reason *increases* with age if those faculties are given sufficient use.

Older people cannot cope with change.

They give up jobs, a way of life, move to a different community or into a smaller house. These changes are greater than those faced by many younger men and women.

Most men and women over sixty-five have no sexual interest or activity.

"Approximately 60 percent of married couples remain sexually active to age seventy-five," says gerontologist Edward W. Busse. For many, sexual interest and activity continue into their eighties and beyond. Lessened sexual capacity often is psychological, caused entirely by current beliefs of society. Elderly men and women who would like to continue sexual activity frequently feel that society disapproves, so they stop. "Let *your* biology, not your neighbor's, be your guide," urges one authority.

All older people are alike.

The aging process spans two and three generations. The differences in characteristics and needs are as great between sixty-year-olds and eighty-year-olds as the differences among any other age categories.

Old age is a disease.

No one dies of old age, according to the AMA's Committee on Aging. "There is no such disease," says *Prevention* magazine. "What we do die of is some infection or degeneration of a vital organ. The more we use every muscle, organ and gland—the more we use our minds—the less likely they are to deteriorate."

Physical limitations imply an inability to function.

A disability need not be a handicap. Many older people adjust to biological changes normal to the aging process and continue to function as vital, interesting men and women.

Admittedly, our culture thrives on youth, but that is no reason for us to be insensitive to the aged among us—to the often harsh reality of their lives, to their needs, to their dreams.

How long are we willing to tolerate the abuse of older, vulnerable people for the sake of avoiding the inconvenience and cost of caring for them properly?

What is it that compels us to discard virtually anything that is old—including human beings—as if the signs of age mark one worthless?

Why do we place so little value on that one quality that only an older individual can offer: wisdom gained from decades of experience and contact with several generations?

When will we begin to devise an intelligent, compassionate and comprehensive approach to the elderly among us?

"In the country of the young, old people move like shadows," notes the *Vista Volunteer*. "They have preceded us as travelers in the land of youth, but we rarely stop to ask them the way. To remember that they were young is to realize that we will be old."

A witness before our U.S. Senate Special Committee on Aging put it more tersely one day: "If you don't die young, you are liable to get old; and if you get old, you had better think about what's going to happen to you."

2.

A WAITING UNTAPPED RESOURCE

Neither one contributes to the Gross National Product. Each is on the fringe of a society that is indifferent to him. One is seventy-four. The other is fourteen. One, a former factory worker. The other, a profoundly retarded and physically handicapped boy.

The teenager is helpless. He does nothing for himself. He does not speak. He makes no response when spoken to. Although the world of the retarded has yet to be mapped, defined by science, it is assumed he will never do these things.

But it also had been assumed he would never walk. And the pair—the factory worker and the retardate—worked together patiently for twelve months and now the fourteen-year-old walks.

9

One measures progress in inches when one works with the profoundly retarded. Louis Schlosser, assigned in effect by the federal government to work with Danny at the Woodbridge (New Jersey) State School, is content to measure in inches.

The sight of deeply retarded teenagers often is a painful one. Because they are in essence children, they act as children do. It is wrenching to see a nineteen-year-old try to chew food and lose half of each spoonful onto his shirt, or to see another, pants dropped, trying to reach the bathroom, or watch a third stare at a magazine that he holds—upside down. It is hard to talk to "empty" eyes, to answer a question which, when answered, is immediately asked again.

But retardation, we are learning, is not unalterable. The capacity of a retarded child can be changed, up or down, within limits, depending on the way he or she is treated. Intelligence is influenced by practice and training just as it is enhanced, or limited, by inheritance, illness, injury or environment. Not infrequently, retarded children do climb, do grow intellectually, do even join the rest of us who lead normal, working, loving lives.

As the nation aimed toward a "great society" under Lyndon Johnson, some ideas took. Why not, it was suggested then, match low-income elderly with children who need help? Foster Grandparents was born. It is an adornment on our society.

At Woodbridge, a home for 1,000 profoundly retarded and severely handicapped children and adults, distinct gains are reported. "My boy," says one Foster Grandparent, "paid attention to nothing. He'd sit all day in his wheelchair and chew on his clothes. Now he doesn't do that anymore. When Friday comes and I'll be gone for two days, he knows it and reacts by hugging and kissing me."

"Jack can't talk, but he can understand me now," reports another. "He'll murmur if he wants something. He'll open his mouth if he's thirsty. He'll pull on my sleeve if he has to go to the bathroom."

"The most depressing part of this job is so often not knowing if you're really making an impression on their lives," says supervisor Ed Guz. "So very few can communicate. But you read to them, you talk to them. You never know what's going on inside the heads of these children, but you've got to believe they appreciate what you're doing even if they can't say so. So you try."

They try: During the past year, ten of the eighty-two children who have Foster Grandparents moved from virtual inactivity into a formal classroom on the grounds.

Louis Schlosser enters Cottage Number Two at Woodbridge each morning by a side door, hoping to be able to hang up his coat before any of the children see him. He fails. "Louie." The call starts in one young throat. Instantly, from every corner of the room, "Louie, Louie . . ." Many of the calls are formless, the name more a cry than a recognizable word. Mr. Schlosser detours into the main room carrying his coat. He goes to each of the fifty-three boys in the cottage, touches each, calls each by name. It takes time because he speaks to each, but he gets to every one. Not an articulate man among adults—he is an immigrant to this country and English is a third, late-acquired language—Louis Schlosser communicates well in Cottage Number Two.

Foster Grandparents complement a paid, full-time staff. Each grandparent is assigned two children and allowed to help in any way he chooses. Because each can work only four hours a day, most of the grandparents give each child two hours. Mr. Schlosser somehow manages to do something for all the boys in the cottage—comb their hair, read a story—in addition to spending time with his two "grandchildren," Danny and Hugh. Hugh is seventeen. To a casual eye, he could be half that. With both boys, Mr. Schlosser does what any parent, or grandparent, would do. He gives them attention.

If they haven't been dressed by the time he arrives, he helps them and then feeds each. If the day is nice, he will take first one, then the other, outside in a wheelchair. Or he will sit and talk to them. If a television program is on, he will wheel the boys closer to the set and then explain what's happening in the show. He talks in adult fashion. He gets no visible response. But he tries, repeatedly. Later he will feed lunch to each. Meals are a torturous process; each tiny mouthful takes about a full minute before it is swallowed. (A major problem at the school—and occasional cause of death—is choking. Because the grandparents have time to feed their children patiently, the incidence of choking has fallen dramatically.) Mr. Schlosser waits. He coaxes. He tells little jokes and stories to "his" boys. He makes sure each eats a substantial amount before he ends the meal.

Mr. Schlosser tried to adopt Danny, to bring him into the small apartment he shares with his wife. The fact that he is white and Jewish and Danny is black and Protestant did not concern him. His request was turned down. The reason: Danny has parents.

Mr. Schlosser quit his job on the assembly line in a candy factory six years ago when he heard of the Foster Grandparent program to be started at the newly constructed state school. He is a charter member of the group.

Eleven thousand Foster Grandparents now work in all our states. All must be sixty or older and earn less than $2,800 a year to qualify. Each is paid $1.60 an hour and receives $1 a day to cover transportation. Forty-eight grandparents work at Woodbridge; a waiting list holds thirty more names. Turnover is slight and usually results from illness or moving.

"Most of our grandparents would become volunteers here if Foster Grandparents ended," says Ed Guz. "They take their children's dirty clothes home to wash personally. They 'visit' on week-ends. They adjust their vacation scheduling for the children's sake. These unfortunate children give the grandparents a necessary love."

Louis Schlosser agrees. "I'd be dead by now if it wasn't for these boys. I feel twenty years younger since coming here. I couldn't give up these kids for anything."

Asked, when he became Danny's grandparent, if he wanted to read the child's medical report, Mr. Schlosser said, "No, I don't need that." He worries about the everyday problems of the two boys. He worries on weekends and holidays when he doesn't see them. He is irritated by the rule that allows a grandparent to work only four hours a day, five days a week.

He made one entry into the "political" arena. In 1972, when the federal government was thinking of cutting $3 million from the Foster Grandparent program, he encouraged all the Woodbridge grandparents to write protest letters to Washington. The budget was ultimately doubled to $25 million.

Louis Schlosser, seventy-four, who has held a number of the anonymous jobs that American industry requires, who worked until he was sixty-eight, makes it clear that he regards what he is now doing as the pinnacle of his life. He refused to move from an inadequate apartment to a better one at a substantial saving in rent because he then would not be able to commute to Woodbridge. He waited four years for an apartment closer to the school. While he waited, this man, who lives on $136.20 a month, spent $2 daily to travel to and from the school.

It took Mr. Schlosser one year to help Danny learn to walk. "I told Danny he had to learn how to walk because soon it'll be me in the wheelchair and I'll expect him to be pushing me around." Mr. Schlosser and Danny have much in common. Both lead simple lives with no frills, no "extras." After five years, there is a visible bond between them, a bond that says, "I need you."

"We are fools when we don't realize all that our elderly can do," says Woodbridge superintendent Louis Pirone. He chafes at the income regulation that prohibits hiring grandparents who earn more than $2,800. "What difference does it make if an elderly man or woman who doesn't need the money wants to help? We have hundreds of children here. There's work enough for all." Foster Grandparents is one of four federally-supported efforts to tap the potential of America's hidden resource of 20 million elderly men and women. (I discuss these programs fully in the Action Resource Guide.) Yet only about 125,000 persons will be able to take part in all four if present administration money proposals are approved. Out of a total national budget of some $300 billion for 1974–1975, we ought to be able to find more than $44 million for these four extraordinarily useful, and proved, programs.

"If everyone could see what our grandparents, more than half of them over sixty-five, do with these children, stereotypes of elderly people would disappear," says supervisor Guz. "What a resource our elderly men and women are, what potential they have—in the community and in the nation."

3.

THE GOLDEN YEARS ON $177 A MONTH

I was introduced to "aging" when I was fifteen. It was during the Great Depression and my father was the cashier of a small neighborhood bank in Chicago. The bank failed. An Illinois law said that anyone holding stock in a bank that failed was liable to depositors for double the amount of his stock. My father not only lost his job, but as a small stockholder in the bank he was personally liable for a debt. Eventually he was forced into bankruptcy.

Although only in his forties, and with considerable experience in both banking and accounting, he could not get a job.

He wrote to more than fifty companies in search of employment. Those who bothered to reply all said essentially the same thing: We don't hire anyone over forty; we have younger people applying for jobs here; you're too old.

At an age when my father had at least two decades of work ahead of him, he felt humiliated as he read those letters. He attempted selling cars and insurance and working in a paint store (which also was forced out of business). Finally he realized that he was unable to provide for his family, and he had to go on relief—the Depression equivalent of welfare.

I have never forgotten the impact on my father. He was deeply ashamed that he had become in part a public charge.

At an early age, I learned what it is to lose control of your life—and something about a society that would so casually deprive someone who had worked so hard and contributed so much for so many years of his dignity.

Within a year, our family worked itself off relief. My mother baked cookies and tarts which I sold door-to-door, and my father found a job as a night clerk at a hotel—seven nights a week, twelve hours a night, for $35. I don't believe anyone who has been even relatively poor can forget it. I know I can't. And our family was comparatively young and healthy when my father lost his job. How much more difficult to be poor *and* old.

In Miami Beach, where a majority of the residents are sixty-five or older, shoplifting in food stores has become so rampant that the local chairman of the Congress of Senior Citizens was moved to remark, "There should be some other way to make ends meet." Of eighty-nine people arrested for shoplifting in one period, "the great, great majority were elderly people," the police chief reported.

The security chief for Grand Union stores told a reporter, "Some of the older women put little packages of meat in their bras. They steal just what they need at the moment: a can of tuna, a bottle of vitamins, some patent medicine."

What does it mean to be over sixty-five today in our country? For too many men and women who have worked hard all their lives and saved for their retirement, it means lack of sufficient money to enjoy those later years. Most of these men and women worked hard until age or disability forced them to stop. A huge number of elderly Americans become poor *only after they become old.* A social worker in Albuquerque says, "One-third of our aged here are forced on welfare for the first time in their lives because they've used up all of their resources. Frequently illness wiped out whatever savings they had.

"Perhaps even more sad," she adds, "are the men and women who refuse to apply for welfare, even food stamps, although they're eating only once a day. They've supported themselves and their families all their lives; they refuse to ask for what they consider to be charity—even if they have to cut down on food and medicine."

A welfare aide in New Jersey wrote, "These are very independent, very proud people and it's difficult to convince them to go on welfare. Some feel it would be a stigma. They spent their whole lives fending for themselves and now they don't want to feel dependent. It's hard to break old habits; they wonder what the neighbors will think."

Eva Raiser, seventy-six, worked much of her life as a registered nurse. Now blind in her right eye and with most of the vision gone from her left, she is generally confined to her small, barren New York City apartment.

Miss Raiser's total income is $78 a month from Social Security. Her monthly rent is $71. An older sister sends her $30 each month. Her balance after rent—$1.23 a day.

She refuses to ask for welfare or even to accept occasional free lunches at a nearby center for the elderly. "I've never taken anything for nothing before," she says. "I don't see why I should start now."

She is legally blind, but says, "I am not going to be considered disabled. I don't want that money." She will not join the new federal Supplemental Security Income program "because it's just another name for welfare. I know I'm foolish. But I just can't ask for welfare or disability aid. If you take away my dignity, what will I have left?"

Twenty-six percent of a group of men and women over sixty-five who were surveyed in Chicago didn't have enough money for food and clothing; yet only 5 percent of them had applied for welfare.

New York City reported that several hundred thousand elderly men and women eligible for welfare assistance refuse it. Much of the reason, according to the city's welfare chief, is pride.

All feel very much like the woman who told the *Los Angeles Times* why she didn't want welfare: "I don't want any part of them or their forms and their questions. Why should I have to go through that to keep a house I worked thirty-five years for? Go down to those places and see the way they treat people. It's an insult. I just want to get my $77 a month in Social Security."

Early in my Senate career, I concluded that there is no substitute for adequate income if we hope to solve some of the most acute problems of the elderly. And aside from an individual's personal income and savings, I believe that only Social Security benefits can satisfactorily provide that income.

Welfare payments can help keep an elderly person adequately fed, clothed and sheltered, but to millions of older citizens, after decades of honest hard work and self-sufficiency, welfare comes as a slap in the face. While it provides a measure of material support, it simultaneously undermines an essential sense of personal dignity.

That is one reason why, in the eight years I have been in the Senate, we have increased Social Security benefits six different times. Since 1969, those raises have meant an overall increase of nearly 70 percent. And although a 70 percent increase is a substantial one, it is simply not enough. Not when one of every five men and women over sixty-five has to live below the poverty level. Not when almost six of every ten widows over sixty-five live in poverty. Not when the average Social Security benefits for millions of older Americans, even with the recent increases, fall below the federal government's poverty line.

Social Security is the economic base for most older Americans. It provides more than half of the income for nearly all elderly couples and for two-thirds of those older people who live alone. Yet in spite of congressional efforts to improve Social Security benefits, the average monthly benefit for a widow of a worker is $177; for a retired worker, $181; for a couple, $310.

By tying Social Security benefit raises to increases in the cost of living index, Congress, with President Nixon's strong backing, took a worthwhile step to upgrade benefits. In addition, the guarantees under the new Supplemental Security Income program (which has taken over welfare payments for the aged poor, among others) now provide at least $146 a month to an individual, $219 to a couple (for those who will accept welfare). But we are still just putting patches on a leaky system. The piecemeal approach to reform of the nation's Social Security and welfare system is producing a hodgepodge of changes, some good and some inadequate. Income problems of the aged poor will not be ended until we redesign the present system.

The inequities, gaps and instances of inadequate planning are many. Just a few examples:

• Retirement results in a sudden, sharp income drop for millions of men and women. Public programs of old-age assistance, together with private pensions or individual savings, seldom yield enough retirement income to replace a significant proportion of pre-retirement take-home pay. Some retired persons have to exist on less than one-quarter of their pre-retirement income.

• It makes no sense that a person can retire at sixty-five, continue to have an income of $100,000 a year in, say, interest and dividends and receive full Social Security benefits. But a man or woman sixty-five or older who is still working can claim all of their Social Security only if they earn less than $2,400. Above $2,400, they lose $1 of Social Security for each $2 they earn.

• Men and women who work past age sixty-five also continue to have Social Security taxes deducted from their pay checks. So, once again, elderly Americans are compelled to pay a special price for working. The system clearly penalizes work.

The time has come for the nation, working through the Congress, to set as a goal the elimination of poverty among our elder citizens. The time has come for Congress to take some significant steps toward achieving this goal.

I am not suggesting that the U.S. Treasury assume the responsibility of issuing monthly checks to every retired person to maintain his income at pre-retirement levels.

I *am* suggesting that more can be done to help each elderly individual obtain a decent retirement income or, for those still in their productive years, to plan for their own financial well-being during retirement.

Individuals must plan for retirement and not rely solely on government to fulfill their every need. It is tragic that many do not—or cannot—prepare for the sudden loss of wages that comes with retirement. Few do anything more than pay Social Security taxes. But Social Security benefits were not designed to be a person's sole means of support during his or her retirement years.

Yet there are things Congress can do.

I think it is reasonable for Congress to establish an interim goal of assuring retired persons an income that is above the poverty line and, in most cases, not less than 50 percent of their incomes in the years before retirement. The Social Security Administration estimates that this goal is reasonable. If we include the Social Security increases of 1970 and 1972—but not the increases of 1974—the Social Security Administration estimates that the median retirement income for men today is about 42 percent of their pre-retirement income and about 50 percent for women.

I believe Congress should set up a longer-range goal of finding ways to assure retired men and women an income that will allow them to retain their pre-retirement command of goods and services. One authority estimates this level of income will have to equal 70 to 80 percent of pre-retirement income, depending upon the income levels of people while they worked.

We should recognize the burden that present federal income tax laws place on the elderly and rewrite the provisions that create those burdens.

Perhaps we should provide men and women over sixty-five with a triple personal tax exemption rather than a double exemption, full deduction of medical expenses and a full tax credit for all Social Security taxes they pay.

I think the present retirement tax credit is unnecessarily complex and an outdated way of reducing the federal tax burden on the elderly. In place of this tax credit—a credit used, incidentally, only by about 50 percent of those who are eligible for it—I prefer a deduction from taxable retirement income of an amount up to the average sum of Social Security benefits paid nationwide during each year. An elderly taxpayer would subtract the total of his own Social Security benefits from the national average to determine the amount by which he may reduce his taxable income. If his own Social Security benefits exceed that average, he would get no credit. But every retired man and woman in the nation would be guaranteed the possibility of a non-taxable amount of income at least equal to the national average Social Security payment.

Older men and women who want to work should be permitted to earn as much as they can and want without restriction. The limitation which now forces loss of Social Security income should be phased out over ten years. This limitation is perhaps the greatest obstacle to an adequate income for many thousands of retired Americans.

After paying Social Security taxes for thirty years or more, people quite properly resent not receiving benefits even if they continue to work. Ending the earnings limitation would encourage men and women over sixty-five who want and need work to feel useful and to lift their standard of living. There is no reason why a man and a woman who have worked full time should, at the moment of a sixty-fifth birthday, have to become part-time employees just to keep their incomes below a government-imposed, totally arbitrary figure.

Years of poverty, hardship and deprivation can be avoided through proper planning for retirement by every individual and by society.

We need a National Commission on Retirement

Income. Among other assignments, the Commission would suggest methods to Congress to achieve our goal of income security for the elderly through maximum use of private pension, annuity and individual savings programs in combination with Social Security benefits and, if necessary, Supplemental Security Income. At least two of the Commission's seven members should be recipients of Social Security or Supplemental Security Income.

Relatively unnoticed, a new class of "elderly" poor is in the making—able, willing workers in their forties, fifties, and sixties who are being kept out or eased out of the job market.

Discrimination against older workers, although forbidden by law, still exists. One Senate study noted that more than 40 percent of the job openings examined restricted employment to workers under age forty-five. At the same time, according to the Senate Special Committee on Aging, many middle-aged and older workers are finding themselves involuntarily (and illegally) retired because of subtle or overt acts of age bias. Forced early retirement is making idle many Americans who are as young as fifty.

The number of unemployed workers over age forty-five hovered near the 1 million mark throughout 1973, a jump of 50 percent in four years. Almost 800,000 men and women between the ages of forty-five and sixty-four withdrew from the labor force during the year. In frustration at their inability to find work, they quit looking. They joined 13.5 million men and women in the same age range already out of the labor force. If just one-fourth of this latter group want jobs, that would raise *real* unemployment for those above forty-five to some 2 million. In sharp contrast, 2 million new jobs opened up during 1973 for men and women under forty-five.

Unhappily, the U.S. has yet to develop a clearcut, effective policy to help middle-aged and older workers who are being kept out of work. Fewer than 5 percent of all new enrollees in manpower and training programs are forty-five or older.

Older Americans don't want charity. But they do need greater income security through expanded employment opportunities. The U.S. Employment Service should give special emphasis to counseling and placement services for older workers. It should vigorously seek out job opportunities for these men and women. Each state office should have a person who specializes in employment problems of older workers.

Age discrimination in hiring can be sharply reduced. The Civil Rights Act of 1964 could and should be amended to prohibit age discrimination in employment. The Equal Employment Opportunity Commission must cooperate with the Secretary of Labor and other public officials to eliminate age discrimination in public and private employment. Employers who receive federal money in any form can be persuaded to do their share in hiring older workers. Each of these points—the National Commission on Retirement Income, the variety of income tax relief measures, the phasing out of the Social Security earnings limitation, the employment aids for older workers and the strengthening of barriers against age discrimination—was included in legislation I proposed to Congress in Spring 1974. They were among a comprehensive set of eight proposals, each designed to promote income security for our elderly.

Each of these programs, if approved by Congress, will cost money, though almost all of them would return to society handsome financial and human dividends. For example, the proposals concerning full tax credit for medical expenses and Social Security taxes, and the reforms I propose in the retirement tax credit, would cost the United States about $500 million a year in lost revenue. The effort to stiffen age-discrimination barriers in employment is estimated at $3 million annually. The bolstering of employment aid to older workers would add about $1.5 million a year to our national tax bill. If the present earnings limitation is completely ended by 1984, the gross cost is estimated at $4 billion a year from that point on; however, this would be offset by taxes paid on earned income and the value of the additional goods and services produced.

We already have seemingly impossible choices to make each year among priorities in our national budget. These proposals are costly and clearly could not all be implemented at once. But we must begin to implement them now if we hope to provide adequate income security for millions of older Americans.

And, let us bear in mind, the taxes paid by the men and women these proposals would help—through new-found employment or departure from welfare rolls—could go a long way in off-setting initial dollars expended.

Twenty million Americans are sixty-five or older now; 42 million more are between forty-five and sixty-five. These two age groups now make up more than one-quarter of our total population.

"In terms of sheer numbers, retirement or the prospect of retirement should be regarded as a major social force in the U.S. today," concluded the Senate's Special Committee on Aging.

"The present system of compulsory retirement from faithful employment solely on the basis of chronological age is completely unrealistic and should be abandoned," says Dr. Irving Wright, clinical professor of medicine at Cornell University's Medical College. "We must provide older people with an opportunity for work commensurate with their abilities rather than with their years."

"Someone is retired because he had too many birthdays," says gerontologist David A. Peterson. "It doesn't matter if he's doing the job well or if he's never done the job well. It's another arbitrary variable."

My own feeling is that a desire or a willingness to retire at sixty-five can be a positive step toward a new, and important, part of one's life. Those who ordinarily plan ahead in their lives, who lead a well-balanced life, including a full range of activities beyond their work, are frequently the very men and women who are anxious to retire and are well-prepared to do so. Employers can help by doing much more than merely informing workers about their pension rights or warning them of some of the difficulties inherent in retirement. Men and women who have worked all their adult lives must be helped to look ahead psychologically to retirement.

When I became president of Bell & Howell in 1949, I decided that a comprehensive retirement program was necessary, one that began well ahead of mandatory retirement age and included counseling and discussion groups in a wide variety of areas, ranging from "The Physical Side of Aging" to "The Meaning of Work and Retirement." These discussion groups were available to our employees and their spouses at age fifty-five.

We allowed voluntary retirement at age sixty with full benefits. Retirement was set at sixty-five, but exceptions were made on a year-to-year basis for some employees up to age sixty-eight. They also took a month's unpaid leave in addition to the regular, paid vacation during their sixty-fifth year; two months unpaid leave plus regular vacation during their sixty-sixth year and three months unpaid leave plus vacation during their sixty-seventh year. The purpose was to give these men and women time to prepare for retirement—both to experiment with retirement activities that attracted them and, for many, a chance to experiment with retirement in other parts of the country.

An inadequate Social Security system; a dehumanizing welfare program; discrimination against older workers; forced, arbitrary and often early retirement—these things increasingly mean that to be old in America is to be poor.

Eighty-eight percent of the Illinois delegates to the 1971 White House Conference on Aging told me, by means of a questionnaire I sent them, that inadequate income is the most serious problem they face.

Inflationary impact is almost calculatedly cruel in the areas most important to the elderly. What's happened to the man or woman who retired as recently as

January 1969 with just enough income to live on? Food has gone up 44 percent; hospital charges, 70.5 percent; medical care, 30 percent; and property taxes, 35 percent. Since 1957-59, hospital charges have jumped 204 percent; property taxes, 180 percent. When this kind of financial pressure is put on a fixed budget, it doesn't take long for the savings account of a lifetime to be wiped out.

"Taxes and surtaxes are making terrible inroads on the retirement income that I worked for so long— an income I have only because of many years of self-denial," a retired teacher told me. "It isn't fair. I should be able to enjoy the monetary security that I worked and planned for."

What do these pressures do to the men and women who have worked all their lives only to discover that financial security eludes them in their later years? According to the Select Committee on Nutrition and Human Needs, it means that increasing millions of Americans are becoming malnourished. It means that many can't, as one woman told me, "enjoy the odds and ends of life—a rare dinner out in the most inexpensive of restaurants." They can't have the periodic health examinations basic to preventing many chronic ills, can't go to movies, buy new clothes, ride public transportation.

In this nation, in this year, there is no way for millions of men and women to finish their lives with a measure of dignified comfort.

4.

FOOD: A MATTER OF SURVIVAL

The line begins to form at about ten-thirty every morning in front of the cafeteria in downtown Albuquerque.

By eleven, when the doors open, the line stretches down the block. The men and women in the line look, and act, remarkably alike. They are at least in their sixties, but most are much older. Their clothes show signs of wear. They don't talk much, and many stare vacantly ahead.

But below the surface signs of age—gray hair and physical infirmity—lies a common malady. As the cafeteria manager explains, "It's their first meal of the day. These people are hungry."

All of them are retired. To avoid breakfast, they sleep late. For many, the cafeteria meal—rib eye steak, two vegetables, salad, all the rolls and coffee they want for $2.19—is their only meal of the day. A snack at bedtime completes the food they'll eat that day.

They don't visit the cafeteria daily. They can't afford it. So they come two or three times a week. The other days, they sleep late and then eat a much smaller combination breakfast and lunch at home.

A former schoolteacher and his wife who eat at the cafeteria earn a total pension income of $175 a month. He has had to take a job as the evening and weekend answering service for a local charity to earn another $25 a week. He and his wife also have made room for boarders in their private home. Both are anemic and should eat large amounts of protein to stay healthy. But they can't afford it.

Food becomes an expendable item when fixed costs such as rent or taxes rise. Accompanied one day by Senator George McGovern, chairman of the Senate's Select Committee on Nutrition and Human Needs, I visited an eighty-seven-year-old woman in East St. Louis and asked her how frequently she was able to eat meat. "Meat," she said. "Why, Senator, I can't remember when I have been able to afford meat. We have chicken wings a couple of times a week and that's it."

"Our older persons are in the midst of a hunger crisis," Jack Ossofsky, executive director of The National Council on the Aging, told the Senate Select Committee on Nutrition and Human Needs. "We are far from a solution of the problem of the nutritional needs of the elderly."

Dr. Albert Klinger, a physician with many patients in Woodlawn, a poor neighborhood of Chicago, told the Senate Committee: "Many of my patients are on a near-starvation diet. They are dying by inches."

Margarita Riaz, seventy-three, who lives in New York City, has $2.10 a day to spend for food. Diabetes has blinded her right eye and has begun to affect her left one. Essential to the control of diabetes are carefully selected foods eaten at specified times. Miss Riaz was told by a physician and a nutritionist at a nearby clinic to eat for breakfast a half pint of milk, an egg, half a grapefruit, two slices of bread and coffee with cream. "I eat a piece of toast, maybe two, some butter and a glass of juice."

Miss Riaz does no better at dinner. She should eat three ounces of meat, chicken or fish, a vegetable, a half pint of milk, a slice of bread and dessert of fruit or custard. "What I usually have is some milk, maybe some meat two or three times a week. When I don't have meat, I'll have an egg or a piece of cheese. Sometimes I just have a lot of oatmeal or dry cereal.

"When I have meat, it will be one small piece. If I have chicken, it will be one piece so I can stretch the package over a couple of meals. Many times I'm still hungry. When I am, I can't fall asleep. I buy four small rolls a week. They stop the hunger pains."

Her daily diet totals about 700 calories—not counting the high-calorie, high-starch, low-nutrient bread, rice and potatoes she often eats to fill her stomach. She is five feet, four inches tall and weighs 183 pounds. Her obesity, a result of the high-starch diet, disguises malnutrition—and has led to hypertension, a form of heart disease. The menu plan of 1,500 calories in selected foods is ignored. The kind of food she eats not only threatens her life by exacerbating her diabetes and hypertension, but it leaves her open to a variety of other, allied diseases.

The nutritionist who gave Miss Riaz the diet to follow says, "We explain how to use the diet and we give shopping advice. There are many cases in which people must eat properly or suffer the health consequences, but they can't because they can't afford to. What can *we* do?"

Miss Riaz no longer visits the nutritionist. "I can't pay attention to the diet they gave me so why should I go? I can't afford what they told me to eat. I know I should be eating a more balanced diet, but I have to buy more potatoes and rice to give me more to eat. I know I'm sick. If I had the money, I'd buy better meats, more chicken and fruit. But five pounds of rice lasts me a couple of weeks."

No nutrition program for the elderly exists where Miss Riaz lives. Her only assistance is food stamps. Because of her net monthly income and other resources, she is eligible to buy $46 worth of stamps each month for $11. But the local food stores know that welfare checks and food stamps arrive by mail at the beginning and middle of each month, so many of the stores raise prices two or three cents on almost all of their items at that time. Elderly men and women don't have the money to stock up on food. They have to buy immediately. They lose a lot of the advantage of the food stamps because of the temporary increase in prices. "I've walked seven blocks to save four cents," says Miss Riaz.

She understands what her food intake is doing to

her health. She has been helped by food stamps and welfare—she probably would have died without them—but vast holes in the system prevent her from living at a level above subsistence.

The extraordinary leap in food costs in 1974—and since 1967 cumulatively—has had a disastrous effect on the poor of all ages. Inevitably, the elderly poor are hit hardest. Since 1967, the cost of poultry has jumped 244 percent, with pork loin up 212 percent, pork sausage up 209 percent and beef up 75 percent. Faced with this kind of inflation, the poor can do only two things: eat less and eat cheaper, less nutritious foods. "No nationwide estimate of the extent of hunger caused by rising food prices is available, but medical experts and local officials in many areas believe it is significant," reports the Select Committee on Nutrition and Human Needs.

The poor, estimates Walter Heller, chairman of the American Economics Association, spend about half of their total income for food, an extraordinarily disproportionate amount of a family's budget. And they still cannot eat the minimum daily amounts of nutrients required to stay well.

How good are government efforts to reach and help the elderly poor? Not very. The National Council on the Aging in 1969 surveyed twelve typical cities. Of 44,000 men and women interviewed, 24,000 were poor. Only 20 percent of them had ever received any government nutrition aid. "It is figures like these," said the American Friends Service Committee, "that make the concerned very angry when the Department of

Agriculture announces that it has returned money appropriated to food programs as 'unused' in order to demonstrate 'fiscal responsibility.' "

How can we do an effective job of meeting the nutrition needs of the elderly? We have made several small beginnings. In addition to the recent Social Security increases, obviously not sufficient because so many of our older men and women still live below the poverty line, the federal government has tied a food stamp program escalator to the cost of food in the marketplace. This stamp allotment is adjusted twice a year to reflect price realities.

We are helping to provide hot, balanced meals in group settings and delivering meals to shut-ins. I will discuss these two efforts, their expansion and their cost fully in the next chapter.

We should amend the Food Stamp Act to deal with the problems of the elderly poor. For example, we should devise special allotments for those men and women who must follow medically prescribed diets.

Also we should help assure the elderly an adequate income—income that reaches the elderly poor, as I outlined in Chapter 2, or income in the form of a new food allowance or supplement paid through the Social Security system.

Anything less than that is turning our back.

At hearings in Illinois, one elderly witness told me, "We do not buy the most nutritious food. We buy the kind we can afford. Dog food is not poison. It tastes good. It has a lot of protein and costs about 39 cents a can. Go into any supermarket in poor areas and ask an old woman, as I did, why she is buying ten cans of dog food. She replied, 'I feed my dog.' I told her that it doesn't taste bad. She hesitated, then agreed. That was the give-away that she was eating it."

Good nutrition is the best form of preventive medicine. "When poor nutrition exists and persists in older adults," a gerontologist told the Senate Select Committee on Nutrition and Human Needs, "it intensifies the severity of other conditions that accompany the processes of aging. By not specifically dealing with the problems of adequate diet in the elderly, we encourage the spiral of chronic disease, physical and psychic disability and ultimate institutionalization."

Aging men and women frequently tell me one of their greatest fears is the possibility of senility. But some nutritionists argue that a proper diet delays or even prevents senility. "There is adequate evidence," says Margaret L. Summers, executive director of the White House Cottage Senior Citizens Center, Springfield, Illinois, "that senility—whatever that is—can be caused by malnutrition alone; if this is the only cause, the condition is not irreversible."

The impact is deeper. "Half to two-thirds of the deaths of older people in our nation," said Mrs. Summers, "are believed to be caused indirectly by malnutrition."

Sean O'Connell manages a supermarket in Los Angeles. Recently, he watched a man stop at the meat freezer and pick up a $1.90 package of chicken. He put it down, picked it up, put it down again, and finally stuffed it into his pocket and walked away.

O'Connell went over to the man in the crowded store aisle and quietly asked him to come to his office.

"He began to cry right there in the aisle," said O'Connell. "I tried not to embarrass him. He must have been at least seventy years old. All I said was, 'Do you have a moment, sir? I'd like to talk with you.' He knew what I wanted. He began to cry, to say he was sorry, to give me the lousy piece of chicken back. "And *I* felt guilty."

5.

SENIOR CENTERS: SERVING THE INVISIBLE ELDERLY

We as a nation are slowly learning that elderly people, like all human beings, have their own special needs. And we are beginning to try in a number of ways to find those elderly who need help and bring that assistance to them.

The story related to me two years ago by Jesse Green, a retired schoolteacher in Washington, D.C., is a case in point. The national nutrition program that now provides hot lunches for nearly 200,000 elderly men and women was then just an experiment in twenty-one cities. It was in danger of extinction. At the time, Arthur Flemming was chairman of the White House Conference on Aging. I wanted to gain his support for expansion of the program and asked him to accompany me at noontime to several senior centers.

We visited a luncheon group one day and talked with a number of the men and women. I asked one of them, "How much does this meal effort mean to you? Is it really necessary?"

"Senator, this meal is a matter of life and death to me," Mrs. Green replied.

"Let me give you an idea of what I mean," she said. "I live on a fixed income that seems to buy less and less each year. I'm on the fourth floor in a small back room and try to fix up my meals as best I can, but my money doesn't seem to buy enough food to adequately provide for me. When this program started just four blocks from where I live, it proved a godsend. Not only did I get a hot nutritious meal for just 25 cents, but suddenly I had some place to look forward to go each day, some place to dress up for, some folks to visit with.

"Last Wednesday, I didn't feel well, however, and decided to stay in bed. About 12:45, I heard shuffling out on the stairs and then a knock on the door and when I said, 'Come in,' three of my new friends from the center burst in and said, 'Jesse, what are you doing in bed and why aren't you down at the center with us having lunch?'

"I told them I didn't feel well and wanted to stay in bed. One of them said, 'Jesse, you're going to feel a lot worse just staying in bed feeling sorry for yourself. Now get yourself dressed and come along with us and you'll feel a lot better.'

"Senator, by three o'clock that afternoon, while we were sitting around talking and after we had had a good lunch and a good visit, I felt fine and I realized that I had had not only food for my stomach but nourishment for my soul. That's what life is all about, having someone care about you, someone who misses you, someone who wants you; just knowing that did a lot more for me than any medicine could. That's what I mean when I say this program is the difference between life and death because being alone, stuffed away in a dark, unattractive room just feeling sorry for yourself really isn't living at all. It can't be what life is all about. *That's* the difference this program has made to me."

"We have reached the point where the rhetoric of concern and piecemeal action are no longer acceptable," says Jane F. Connolly, director of the Senior Centers of Metropolitan Chicago. "We are beginning to look for the elderly who are ill, who are impoverished, who are isolated. We are finding a way to reach out a hand to all aging Americans wherever they may be, a hand offering a variety of basic services such as food, transportation, companionship."

Senior Centers of Metropolitan Chicago, a private, nonprofit agency, was founded in 1956 as the city's first agency designed solely to provide aid to men and women over sixty. The agency operates four senior centers and has about 1,000 members. Their average age is seventy. Two-thirds of its paid employees are sixty or older. Its financial support comes from the Community Chest and private philanthropic sources.

For these elderly Chicagoans, and thousands of other Americans, senior centers provide an unduplicated variety of services these men and women have come to rely on. But there are simply too few senior centers. The National Council on the Aging says about 200,000 are needed. Only 2,000 centers exist.

Legislation now exists—has, in fact, existed since 1973—that would allow us to move past the rhetoric of concern and piecemeal action and a long way toward the 200,000 centers called for by the National Council on the Aging. That year Congress gave the administration the authority to pay up to three-quarters of the cost of acquiring or renovating existing facilities to serve as multipurpose senior centers. The legislation would provide grants to help the initial staffing of these centers.

This existing legislation could go far toward meeting a vital need of the elderly; depending upon the program devised, it could meet the entire need. As of mid-1974, however, the Department of Health, Education, and Welfare has taken no steps to use this authority to devise any plan.

Miss Martha Herbert, at eighty-six, is kept out of a nursing home by one thin thread: the multifaceted aid she receives from Chicago's Senior Centers. Alert and articulate, she has glaucoma, heart disease and can't move around without a four-legged walker because of a once-broken hip.

"It's utterly impossible for me to stand on my feet long enough to cook. I'm too unsteady. I fear scalding myself." For $11.25 a week, she receives two meals—a hot lunch and cold dinner—delivered to her Monday through Friday by the centers. She must go to a Chicago hospital each month for an examination and medication. "I once tried to get there by taxi. That cost $4.15 and I can't afford that. It's impossible to take a city bus. The stop is two blocks away, and, even if it was right in front of the door, it's impossible for me to climb that big step onto the bus."

The center's minibus service takes Miss Herbert to the hospital and back home. The driver, Mrs. Richard Jones, a full-time employee of the centers, visits briefly with Miss Herbert when she delivers lunch and dinner and returns later to do any necessary chores. She's the only steady contact Miss Herbert has with anyone outside her one-room basement apartment on Chicago's North Side.

Nursing home? Miss Herbert is quick to reject that idea. "I've worked hard all my life"—she did not retire until 68—"and I've never wanted much. But I want something now. I want to stay here. I'm entitled to it." She waves an arm to indicate the 12 × 18-foot room in which she lives. "Here I have my privacy and my freedom. No one tells me what to do. I'm limited, of course, but this is mine. I've always been independent and I hope to remain that way for my remaining years. God willing, I'll stay here."

Many communities deliver meals to elderly men and women who, like Miss Herbert, are homebound. I wanted to see for myself the value of these delivered meals. Thus, unannounced, one day I accompanied Rusty Hodgden, the young driver of a minibus for Chicago's Senior Centers. I walked in and visited with men and women, many in their late eighties, often with broken hips and arthritic legs, men and women who could not get up even to use the stove or the refrigerator. But they wanted to stay in their own homes and out of a nursing institution. The meals delivered daily and the human contact made it possible. For both the recipients of the meals and Rusty, personal needs were satisfied. One elderly man told me: "I look forward so much to this young man coming. He sits down and talks to me for ten or fifteen minutes." As we left, Rusty told me what it meant to him to witness a kind of human need he had never known before, "I feel needed and wanted every day of my life now," he said.

The elderly pay what they can for their meals—10 cents, 25 cents, more if possible. Many of them would not take the meals if they were not allowed to pay whatever they could for them.

The delivered-meals program allows men or women whom the elderly trust to have access to them, to learn when they have problems and to guide them to solutions: to medical attention; to counseling of various sorts; to transportation available to them at reduced or no cost; to Social Security benefits (strangely, thirty-nine years after the introduction of Social Security, several million Americans still do not know when and if they are eligible); to Medicare and Medicaid benefits. Depending on the community, these home-delivered meals are paid for by federal, state or private money.

Another food program, begun in 1968 as an experiment, provides hot meals to the elderly in community centers or other convenient locations. In 1971, we were able to obtain the $1.6 million needed to continue the pilot projects only after a protracted Senate floor fight. This June, however, the Senate unanimously approved a bill introduced by Senator Edward Kennedy and me which extended the Nutrition Program for the Elderly for three more years at a cost of $600 million. By the end of that period, some 400,000 older Americans will benefit from these meals. " . . . Before this program started," wrote *The New York Times*, "many of these old people were suffering from malnutrition. They used to sit alone all day in their separate apartments drinking tea and eating toast, perhaps with cottage cheese or tuna fish. That is all they ever ate because they had no money for food or were too old to cook. Many became ill and had to be put in hospitals or old age homes at public expense. They suffered from ailments real and imaginary and filled the waiting rooms of clinics at public expense. Sometimes they died and their bodies were not discovered for weeks because nobody missed them.

"As a result of the lunch program, the old people get a hot, well-balanced meal every day. Doctors have found that their health has improved. The clinics are less crowded. Senility does not set in as early because the old people have friends now, lunch companions they see every day. They are back in touch with reality."

Of all the efforts this country has conceived to make the lives of our elderly more comfortable and more meaningful, few have had more impact than the hot lunches served in and by the community.

The side benefits seem almost endless. In Seattle, a participant in a nutrition program became ill and was taken to a hospital. A nurse, seeing a membership card, called the local senior center to complain that the man seemed dazed and said they would have to put him into an institution. Fortunately, the nurse was talking to John Gannon, a sixty-seven-year-old employee of the center. He replied tartly: "Has it occurred to you that he is stone deaf?" The man had been in that hospital before. Notation of his deafness was in his records. But no one had bothered to read them.

One eighty-year-old woman, severely handicapped by arthritis, started coming to lunch in Seattle at the insistence of friends. She had to walk four blocks down a steep hill each day to reach the center and was able to manage that only with help. After a snowfall last winter, she had to miss more than a week because it was too dangerous for her to walk that distance. When she returned, she said, "Not only did I miss the good meal and being with everyone, but the walk helped me physically so much I'm going to have to start all over again building myself up."

I've been told that in Seattle many of the women are dressing better, that several romances have begun, that one man who had lost weight gave a handsome coat he could no longer wear to another man who needed a coat.

Nearly 200,000 men and women now participate in this hot lunch program. It costs $100 million a year for meals and other services. This figure will increase to $250 million annually at the end of three years. Yet even that amount apparently doesn't begin to meet the need. Dr. Donald M. Watkin, chief of the nutrition program, has estimated that as much as $2 billion could be used each year if we are to successfully help those elderly Americans who require this kind of food effort. But compare this to the $4.5 billion we paid in 1973 to farmers for *not* growing crops.

We as a nation don't know where all our elderly

poor are, what kinds of help they require or even how many there are. One group that is trying to overcome society's indifference to those who desperately need aid is the Neighborhood Workers of Chicago's Senior Centers. For the past seven years, these twenty-two men and women—all over sixty-five and most of them part-time employees—have sought out the elderly needy and then seen that help was provided.

"The Neighborhood Workers have been the most successful part of our efforts to bring help to the elderly," says Ms. Connolly. "The tangible results produced by these workers, ordinary people with little or no formal training, have astonished professionals. The secret of their success seems to lie in their approach to the job they perform, a job that uses the natural, neighborly impulses of sympathetic people to react as a friend to someone who is alone or in need of help."

The Neighborhood Workers have provided services to the elderly that some government agencies have been unable or unwilling to offer. They have filled a gap. All of them live in the areas in which they work; they know the stores, the streets, the people. Retired teachers, factory workers, domestics, businessmen or housewives, they become almost a substitute family for men and women who often are shut-in and totally alone. Their genuine concern and moral support give the elderly a new stability and chance to break out of isolation.

Mrs. Helene Duffy, seventy-one, visits twenty "friends" a week. (She refuses to call them clients.) All but two are women; several are in their eighties. Most are able to take care of themselves and their apartments. Mrs. Duffy's major job is to be a friend, to help drive away isolation, loneliness, depression. She'll shop for some, look after problems for others, chat with all. Some of the women she visits put on a good dress and make-up that one day each week because Mrs. Duffy is the most important guest they receive.

Rapport usually comes easily. "We've shared many of the same experiences," says Mrs. Duffy. "Most of us are widows and our families have moved away. We have similar economic problems, limited incomes and we all have an uncertain future."

Mrs. Duffy must walk fairly long distances to make visits to four- or five-story walkups—not an easy task for someone seventy-one—yet she has never missed a day of work in six years. "I hope to keep it up for years to come," she says. "Without this work, *I* might be a lost soul.

"So often, the men and women I visit tell me, 'I don't know what I would do without you, Helene.' I accept that not for me but for the Neighborhood Workers and the Senior Centers. It demonstrates that each of my friends knows he or she has a lifeline to the world."

Transportation plays an essential role in the comprehensive programs of many senior centers. Chicago's Centers, aware of the inability of many aged men and women to get around without aid—and the difficult time virtually all the elderly have in coping with standard mass transportation—have a free service that helps the elderly run necessary errands, see physicians, get to center affairs. The service is another one of the integral links that keeps centers like the ones in Chicago functioning.

A growing number of areas are dealing intelligently with this problem. Helena, Montana, has a Dial-a-Bus service. In the four-square-mile area of New York City that is said to have the heaviest concentration of elderly people in the nation, a special reduced-fare Dial-a-Ride taxi service has been started for the old and the handicapped. Newark, New Jersey, used part of a $7 million federal grant designed to improve municipal services to buy ten specially designed sixteen-passenger minibuses to help the elderly and the handicapped reach essential places—including recreational and cultural facilities—without charge.

Men and women who are over fifty-five or handicapped have formed a reduced-fare transportation cooperative in seventeen Missouri counties. Lincoln, Nebraska, provides small buses and vans for the elderly and the handicapped. Two vans have hydraulic wheel chair lifts. In Denville, New Jersey, a sixteen-passenger minibus makes two runs through the township every weekday taking elderly men and women wherever they must go without charge. Asked what this new service meant to her, one woman said, "This is even better than having your own transportation because you get to see your friends and meet people on the bus. When you live alone, you tend to magnify problems. Sometimes, when I feel down, I just get on the bus for the ride and then I perk up again."

"Although concern about the problems of the

aged has accelerated in recent years," says Ms. Connolly of Chicago's Senior Centers, "constructive remedial action has been slow in coming. Legislation lags. For example, more money is available now for programs for the elderly but it is still so little in relation to the need. We are so short of housing for the elderly here that there is about a three-year wait. That's a long wait for an older person. It seems that when legislation *is* passed, it has taken so long in the doing that the need for it has already outstripped the legislative 'solution.'

"Social services remain fragmented. Social workers persist in assigning the elderly a low priority. Many centers cater to the 'well' aged, serving those fortunate few able to attend center functions, and often failing to look beyond their walls to the ill, the impoverished and the isolated—the so-called 'invisible elderly.'

"The talk of 'concern' won't do any longer," she says. "We must work out the many different problems of aging and deliver tangible services—programs like home-delivered meals, Neighborhood workers, free transportation—to all aging Americans who need help wherever they are."

6.

THE COLD SHOULDER OF HEALTH CARE

"We live in a youth-oriented society and many people in our health institutions have no interest in the aged," says Dr. Morton Ward, medical director of the Philadelphia Geriatric Society. "At best, they tend to give poor care."

This professional indifference begins in the medical schools. There is a desperate need for more health personnel in geriatric care. Yet, in fifty-one of ninety-nine medical school catalogues checked, there was no mention of instruction in care of the elderly. Only fifteen of twenty thousand medical school faculty members are identified primarily with the aging. Yet 86 percent of the elderly have chronic illnesses.

"In spite of the fact that the aged account for 24 percent of hospital stays," says Duke

University sociologist Erdman B. Palmore, "they clearly are falling far short of the medical care they need. Though their illnesses are both more prevalent and more severe than those of younger people, they average only about one more physician visit per year."

A study of Social Security recipients in Chicago found fewer than 20 percent had "good health." Yet two-thirds of those who were ill had not talked to a doctor or a nurse in the previous three months. Seventy-six percent should have been taking daily medication; most were not. Palmore reports that among every 100 elderly men and women who were also poor, health aids such as dentures and eyeglasses were needed but were not owned.

The poor who are sick often don't consult physicians until they are severely ill. A hospital in Newark, New Jersey, examined 211 elderly residents of the inner city there and learned that only three were without medical problems. Yet half of them had not seen a doctor in two years. Fewer than one out of ten had received a complete physical examination in that time. Half of the group had heart disease. A quarter suffered from hypertension. Eighteen percent had diabetes. All of these ailments, of course, can kill.

"With the chronically ill aged, medical progress does not come immediately," says the University of Washington's Dr. Carl Eisdorfer. "It is not a matter of days or weeks but of a much longer time, so many doctors shy away. One of the most popular things to do at an out-patient clinic is to refer elderly patients back at a time when someone else will have to see them."

Mrs. Elise Addams, seventy-seven, a life-long resident of New York City, knows firsthand the indifference of many doctors and nurses toward the elderly. She also knows about the bureaucratic hassle and physical hardship often associated with a trip to a hospital or clinic.

A visit to the outpatient clinic at French & Polyclinic Hospital illustrates Mrs. Addams' continuing struggle to obtain adequate health care. Rising early, and walking with the two canes she needs to get around, Mrs. Addams arrived at the hospital's outpatient clinic at 8 A.M. Doctors come at nine-thirty, but Mrs. Addams was told to be there at eight; this was to allow time for her Medicare papers to be processed so the physicians would not be held up. The clerk didn't call her until after nine o'clock. The processing took three minutes.

About an hour later, she was summoned to an examination room. The doctor decided she needed a blood test and an electrocardiogram. Before she could get a blood test, however, she had to obtain clearance from the cashier on the first floor. The clinic is on the third floor. The charge nurse told Mrs. Addams she should have gotten the clearance before she came upstairs. "How could I have gotten clearance for the blood test before I knew I needed one?" Mrs. Addams asked. She went back downstairs. When she returned to the third floor, she was exhausted. "They don't really think about my having a tough time getting around, do they?" she said.

The blood sample was drawn. Mrs. Addams asked about the electrocardiogram. No technician was available to give it. She would have to come back next week, again at eight. This woman with bad feet and bad legs again would have to travel thirty-three blocks to the clinic for a test that takes perhaps five minutes. She didn't protest.

On the way out, she asked for authorization to go to the hospital's dental clinic to have her bottom dentures replaced. That form would simply note there was no medical reason why her teeth could not be worked on. (She had come to the clinic to have the dentures replaced when they broke two months earlier. "The dental nurse wouldn't even let me come in because she said I didn't have a slip from the medical clinic." Not having. been told what to do, Mrs. Addams went home and waited until this second visit two months later to ask for the clearance. In the meantime, she could not eat anything that was too solid.)

Clearance in hand, Mrs. Addams went to the dental clinic, told the secretary there that she had the form and asked to see a dentist. The secretary didn't want to see the clearance, but asked if Mrs. Addams was registered with the dental clinic. Mrs. Addams didn't understand. The secretary told her to come back the following Monday to register. She could not see a dentist on Monday, merely register. Mrs. Addams was about to leave when she remembered seeing a dental notation on her clinic card. She told the secretary, who then looked at the clinic card and said, indeed, Mrs. Addams was registered. The secretary had been too indifferent to ask to see the card in the first place.

Mrs. Addams returned to the clinic the following Tuesday for the electrocardiogram and dental appointment. She got the heart test, but only after waiting two hours needlessly. The receptionist for the unit forgot to tell the charge nurse. ("It's a lack of communication," one nurse said. "Happens here a lot.") After the test, Mrs. Addams asked the findings. Six doctors were on duty in the unit, but she was told she would not receive the results until her next visit. Mrs. Addams finally got her dentures as well, but it took six visits over a three-month period. She went almost a half-year without bottom teeth.

Mrs. Addams and too many like her are treated quickly, sent home and forgotten until the next visit—if they are able to return. But they, the oldest and weakest of our society, must take the initiative. She is asked to make frequent trips to the clinic although each trip is a torment. During one recent month, for example, she had to visit the medical, physiological and nutritional departments, all on different days.

Bureaucratic systems seem to breed indifference in direct proportion to their size and the fragmentation of work assignment. Nowhere is this truer than when the clients are the poor, the aged and the infirm. When Mrs. Addams' examination was finished one day, she was given three pieces of paper, each a different set of instructions. She literally had no idea what each was. When she first started at the clinic, she became lost trying to find the x-ray room. "I wound up spending the whole day walking around that hospital."

She was never told why she had to receive an electrocardiogram. "I leave here not knowing any more than when I came in. The doctors talk right in front of me, but when I ask if they are talking about me, they say no. They never tell me directly. I'm not a charity case. I've paid for my Medicare and I want to be treated nicely."

"When you are sixty-five, you find your complaints are no longer listened to," Sharon Curtin, R.N., testified before the Senate's Special Committee on Aging. "You meet the impenetrable barrier of glazed eyes and careless hands anxious to take care of someone younger, someone who seems to have a higher potential for complete recovery. If you have an ache or a pain, it is because you are old; if you are depressed, it is because you are senile."

Although Mrs. Addams suffers from the widespread bureaucratic insensitivity that typifies our federal Medicare program, Medicare nonetheless was one of the most significant pieces of social legislation in the history of our country. It was a first step toward making health care a right rather than a privilege.

But with the enactment of Medicare in 1965, many were led to believe that all elderly people would be assured quality medical care. They were wrong. Medicare was, and is, a program designed to help the elderly meet some of their medical care costs. It was not set up to improve the health care system. Nor was it intended to provide for all the health care needs of the elderly.

Medicare's tragedy is that its rhetoric outstripped its substance. Its beneficiaries—the nation's elderly—believed its promise and thus felt cheated by its reality.

As inflation worsened and costs rose sharply, that reality became ever harsher; bureaucratic screws tightened, bringing costs in line with the federal budget.

The program's ever-widening gaps have left the elderly spending more of their own money for health needs than they did before 1965, for Medicare is picking up an ever-smaller amount of the elderly's health costs. In 1969, Medicare paid 46 percent of their health bill. In 1974, it paid 42 percent. It will not pay for many health needs, among them drugs, eyeglasses, preventive examinations, custodial and dental services. This imposes a significant hardship on the elderly, who require more long-term—and thus more expensive—medical attention than younger people. The medical bills of an average elderly couple are three times larger than those of a younger couple.

Medicare does allow many persons over sixty-five to cope with daily medical needs and expensive illnesses. "However," says one geriatric specialist, "those on fixed incomes or dependent on Social Security for basic income are in trouble."

The fact that Medicare doesn't pay for drugs, often the major health expense for those suffering from chronic illnesses, is a particular strain. By questionnaire, I asked delegates to the 1971 White House Conference on Aging how they felt about Medicare. Their primary request: Allow Medicare to cover prescription drugs. Many men and women past 65 now must decide daily if they will buy medicine or food.

Nor does Medicare cover the cost of hearing aids. Approximately 20 million Americans suffer from hearing impairment, a great many of whom are over sixty-five. Yet only 2 million Americans own hearing aids. Vast numbers of elderly citizens living on fixed incomes are unable to bear the cost of these sometimes essential aids.

Medicare is viewed by a large number of our elderly as a broken promise and a bureaucratic monster. For one thing, they don't understand what health needs Medicare covers. Many private insurance carriers—which function as intermediaries between the government, those who provide health care, and the elderly—are extremely inefficient.

Confusion over coverage is widespread. Many patients logically believe that whatever treatment is ordered by their physician is essential. Therefore, they assume the treatment must be covered by Medicare. Too often, they may be informed *after the fact* that Medicare refuses payment.

A hospital patient and his wife told me they objected strongly to a treatment recommended by their physician because they were afraid Medicare would not cover it. Both the physician and the local Medicare office said the fee would be paid, so the couple finally agreed. Four months later, the hospital sent them a bill for $3,207. Medicare had refused to pay.

The gaps in Medicare coverage often mean humiliation. "The foot doctor, the eyeglass doctor, they don't work for nothing," says Mrs. Addams. "They make me pay first so they're sure I've got the money."

The "pay first" attitude can be critical. In a number of cities, private ambulance services demand payment before they take an emergency victim to a hospital. "Until we know what charges Medicare will cover," a public aid official in Illinois says, "we are unable to determine who will pay what claim."

The "pay first" syndrome reaches into the doctors' offices. Doctors sometimes ask single office-visit payment of $40 from patients on welfare before they will examine them. "Forty dollars is an outrageous price to begin with," a senior citizens' aide in Detroit said recently, "but to take $40 from an elderly man or woman is often just immoral."

"Urologists taking out prostates and ophthalmologists operating for cataracts have a very good thing going for them," an executive of one of New York City's largest medical centers told *The New York Times*, "just as a Medicare for children would raise the income of pediatricians."

Medicaid also has come under sharp attack. Medicaid is the federally aided, but *state*-designed and -administered program of medical assistance; unlike Medicare, it is a welfare program. Therefore, it is subject to the vicissitudes of social stigma and taxpayers' perennial opposition—and ever vulnerable to budgeting shears. Because of its precarious political position, Medicaid often is forced to pay less-than-adequate prices for frequently less-than-adequate services carried out in many instances by marginal practitioners in marginal facilities.

Without effective quality or cost controls, Medicaid invites rising costs and abuse. Moreover, since the program differs from state to state, Medicaid's variations in coverage, benefits and eligibility requirements have produced gross inequities in the delivery of health services to the poor. It has helped the elderly poor, primarily in covering the gaps left by Medicare, but Medicaid in many ways exemplifies charity medicine at its worst, subjecting its beneficiaries to means tests and "hand-outs" of second-class care that rob them of human dignity.

"It assaults the human condition," says Dr. John H. Knowles, president of the Rockefeller Foundation and a sharp critic of U.S. health care methods, "to have someone come into your home . . . and look under the bed and into the closet to see if there is a television set. Most of the people in this country are not chiselers or deadbeats."

It is long since time to change Medicare from a limited insurance program to one that will provide the elderly with comprehensive assistance, including preventive care, home health care, and coverage of catastrophic health problems.

Filling the gaps left by Medicare, however, will be an expensive proposition. One plan, introduced by Senator Abraham Ribicoff, which would expand Medicare coverage but not eliminate all payments by the beneficiary, would cost about $17 billion a year.

A number of national health insurance proposals designed to adequately finance the health care needs of all age groups have been introduced in Congress. The major proposals—one supported by the administration; another introduced by Senators Russell Long and Abraham Ribicoff and co-sponsored by me; and still another sponsored by Senator Edward Kennedy and Congressman Wilbur Mills—would each cost between $8 to $9 billion a year in additional federal expenditures.

In 1965, it was the undisputed health needs of the elderly that prompted the enactment of Medicare. Now the issue has extended beyond the elderly to include the health care needs of every American. Regardless of age or income, we all have a basic right to competent medical care. The adoption of national health insurance will mean improved access to health care for all Americans.

7.

LOOKING FOR THE HIDDEN PEOPLE: HOME HEALTH CARE

An eighty-four-year-old man was found in an abandoned building, malnourished, confused, suffering from pneumonia. Today, he lives in an apartment building for the elderly, able to care for himself with supervision.

An eighty-seven-year-old woman, living alone, was in a state of panic because she had found a mass in her breast and did not know what to do about it or whom to contact. Now, treated, she is again self-sufficient.

A seventy-eight-year-old woman with chronic heart disease suffered such severe pain that she refused to walk three flights of stairs from her apartment to the street, hence isolating herself. A new live-in homemaker oversees use of medication to reduce the pain and helps diminish her once overwhelming sense of loneliness.

Each of these people was found by an innovative home-health-care team that reaches out to the medically untouched who live in one small corner of New York City—to elderly men and women who are too sick, poor or frightened to seek health care on their own. Their average age: eighty.

The home care unit, based in St. Vincent's Hospital and Medical Center, looks for the hidden people struggling with inadequate incomes who have outlived or have been abandoned by their families and friends. "We want to keep them out of institutions, in their communities adequately housed and as healthy as possible," says Dr. Philip W. Brickner, co-director. "We want to help them retain their independence and their integrity."

The health team brought the eighty-four-year-old man and the woman with the breast lump into St. Vincent's, treated them, then arranged for living quarters for the man and follow-up care for both. The woman with heart pain was treated in her apartment and put on a medical regimen, and the homemaker was hired so she would not have to go to a nursing home.

"These patients were rescued," says Dr. Brickner, "but in our city many other helpless, homebound, aged people remain unsought and unknown. Lack of care for this group—not just medical care—is a serious problem that afflicts American society. It demands immediate attention. We can provide concrete help to a small number; but we hope we can focus attention on the magnitude and complexity of this gap in medical—*human*—services."

St. Vincent's program brings doctors, nurses and social workers to a "melting-pot" area of lower Manhattan that contains about 155,000 persons, many of them low-income aged who live in deteriorated tenement buildings with no elevators and no security, or in single-room occupancy buildings and welfare hotels. All of the members of the team—twelve physicians, fifteen social workers and a large number of nurses and student nurses—are volunteers. They work on St. Vincent's time and with hospital backing. Contributions from neighborhood civic groups allow three additional members to be paid—a secretary and a driver-community worker, both of whom speak Spanish and Italian, and a homemaker. A station wagon saves the cost of an ambulance, a charge that can be as high as $60. The driver is qualified to operate a portable electrocardiograph, donated by St. Vincent's, to allow monitoring in a patient's home.

The community groups help the medical teams find the people in need. No one knows how many aged men and women live in the area, but estimates range as high as 3,000. "So many of the elderly pull into themselves when problems occur," says co-director James Janeski, a social worker. "They lose all contact with other human beings. Finding them is one of our most difficult problems."

"Current hospital and medical practice is based on the premise that the sick person will actively seek out and go to a source of health care," says Dr. Brickner. "When we require the patient to take this initiative, we ignore everyone else who is unable to come to us.

"American medicine is not reaching the isolated, homebound aged. Out of contact with the medical-care system, they are often too disabled or bewildered to seek help. Occasionally, a neighbor may find a failing person and call an ambulance. But it's too late for effective treatment when a patient comes to the emergency room dying or in an advanced stage of disease."

The evidence is clear: extraordinary financial savings—measured for the nation in billions of dollars—would be achieved if a comprehensive program of home care were developed—one that kept the elderly out of hospitals and nursing homes or got them out and back home quicker. The additional importance of allowing the elderly to stay in their homes, where familiar surroundings provide them with a sense of security, is beyond measure.

Although sick elderly people usually prefer to be kept at home—and could be kept there with adequate aid—they are often sent instead to an institution. Unfortunately, home health care—a complex of services which may be used as needed—has a very low priority in the U.S.

As many as 500,000 persons each year are sent to institutions for reasons other than health care. They could be released if they had someone to help them at home. Medicare and Medicaid and private funds pay a minimum of $800 a month in New York to keep these men and women in an institution. But Medicare and Medicaid in most cases will not provide the $10 to $15 a day required for home health care. Less than 1 percent of all money spent through Medicare now goes for home health services and even that amount is dropping—from $79.3 million in 1969 to $61.1 million in 1972. But in one year—1972—Medicare payments to hospitals rose from $5 billion to $5.4 billion.

The patient who needs a variety of home care services is effectively shut out unless he can pay for it himself. Home health policies under Medicare have been so narrowly defined that help in meeting the real need is negligible. Under Medicare, home care is basically confined to skilled nursing services. As a result, home health services have focused to a substantial degree only on acute illnesses.

"The system has a very strong institutionalization bias," reports the Senate Special Committee on Aging. "Medicare will pay for most services in an institution; it won't pay for many in the home." Illinois State Senator John A. Davidson makes the same point: "Our health care system is more interested in illness treatment than health maintenance, and is overly dependent on institutions to which the elderly must reach out rather than on institutions that reach out to the elderly."

Home care can be a major response to rising medical costs. The National Association of Home Health Agencies reports that hospitalization is three and a half times as expensive as home care. The Association estimates that $100 million could be saved each year if the average hospital stay were shortened by just one day.

In a Florida study, physicians said 20 percent of the patients in a nursing home could live in their own homes if home services were available. One man was seen at home daily by a visiting nurse for twenty days. The family paid $252. Medicare did not cover the visits. The hospital cost for the same twenty days, for just the bed, would have been $1,780. Medicare would have paid the whole bill.

An elderly woman in Salt Lake City suffered a stroke with some paralysis and congestive heart failure. Her physician ordered nursing care at home. A home care team devised a program in which it supervised medication, began physical therapy, taught the family how to help, gave nutrition instruction and began bowel and bladder control training. "Within five weeks," our Senate committee was told, "this ninety-year-old lady was walking with the use of a cane, had regained bowel and bladder control and was approaching maximum rehabilitation. Her own determination, an intelligent, involved family and the care provided in just 29 visits by our agency team—nurse, physical therapist and nutritionist—led to this. Total cost: $349.13, paid in full by Medicare and Medicaid because the physician authorized the treatment. A comparable five-week hospital stay would have cost $2,695. A nursing home: $875."

A Massachusetts survey revealed that patients who were paying $500 a month in homes for the aged could receive the necessary nursing, homemaking and food services at home for $160 a month. If enough home aid existed in that one state, the researchers said, 10,000 men and women now in institutions there could go home at once.

"In 1961, the Rochester home care cost was about $8 a day and in 1971 it was $16," says Dr. Charles Weller, of the Rochester (New York) Home Care Association Program. That is $76 a day less than the average daily cost of a hospital bed. In 1970, that one home care program in one city saved more than $1 million.

Medicaid operates a home care plan in Oklahoma that allows 3,000 patients to receive the services they need in their own homes. The help is given by live-in, paid aides who are called Providers. Twenty percent of them are between sixty-six and seventy-five. They are supervised, after initial training, by a team of Registered and Practical Nurses. One elderly man, confined to bed in a nursing home for several years, went home with a Provider. Within months, he was able to walk short distances and had regained an interest in his community. His live-in Provider, for her part, was earning enough money to regain custody of her two small children from a county foster home. The boys had a "grandfather" figure who was loving and supplied discipline; the patient knew he was needed; and the Provider had someone to help her plan for the future.

Any comprehensive health care program must have its roots in preventive medicine. Preventive medicine is especially essential for the elderly, who are known to suffer from diseases that begin slowly and can be prevented or delayed if diagnosis is made early.

The Flannery Clinic in Chicago's Flannery apartments for the elderly is an example of what preventive medicine can accomplish. Located within the apartment complex, it serves residents of the apartments as well as elderly men and women who live nearby. Northwestern Memorial Hospital serves as a back-up, providing treatment the clinic can't handle and inpatient care. Neither the clinic nor Northwestern charges anything beyond Medicare or Medicaid fees. No one is refused aid. By making medical care accessible, the clinic emphasizes early recognition of problems and convenient follow-up examinations—the basis of preventive medicine. Free transportation is provided to Northwestern. Most of the clinic patients visit once a month. The board of directors of the clinic all live in the apartments; they alone determine what the clinic will provide.

Nationally, one out of ten men and women over sixty-five is hospitalized each year. For the elderly it serves, the Flannery Clinic cuts that rate in half.

The Flannery Clinic is one response to the problems of the elderly who are ill. The St. Vincent's program is another. "We've proved that these kinds of programs are effective," says Dr. Brickner of St. Vincent's. "We've devised a method of delivering medical and social services to once-hidden people. We're providing human contact that was once absent from their lives. We know that a substantial number of disabled patients can be helped to maintain an independent life and stay out of institutions if basic services are provided in their homes. To these elderly people, their homes are where they are most comfortable mentally; that's crucial to anyone's well-being."

8.

HOUSING THE ELDERLY: AN AMERICAN FAILURE

I received this letter recently: "I am seventy-four years old and live in a building seventy years old. I moved here six years ago and paid $90 a month for rent. Then the building was sold. The first two years, my rent was raised $5 each year. Then I got a $10 increase. Now, $20 more. I get $141 Social Security. Rent is $130. Plus gas, plus utilities, plus telephone. How can I eat?"

Of all the groups affected by the housing shortage in this country, perhaps the elderly suffer more than any. About one out of three of our elderly men and women—6 million people—live in substandard housing. Apart from the fact that these buildings meet none of the special needs an older person has, many are so badly run down that they preclude a life of even simple dignity.

Our Senate Special Committee on Aging reported that men and women over sixty-five have "limited opportunities to change their housing to suit their needs." Apartments are scarce, and the elderly often are forced to compete for rental with younger men and women who have more money. In times of severe shortage, the elderly are the ones who are forced to accept the rundown apartments that would otherwise be empty. In every city, an increasing—and countless —number of hotels that can't survive as hotels are turned into one-room flophouses for the elderly.

A minimum of 120,000 housing units should be built each year with federal aid for men and women over sixty-five, the 1971 White House Conference on Aging recommended. Our best annual effort to date: 41,000.

In every large city, there are thousands of hidden elderly poor. Rose Mary Wender is one of them.

Miss Wender, an articulate woman of sixty-nine, lives in a dirt-caked, sixty-eight-year-old apartment building in New York City.

Every stairway landing leading to her fifth-floor walk-up apartment is piled so high with garbage that all fire-escape exits are blocked. In the fourteen years Miss Wender has lived there, nineteen fires have broken out on the building. They always occur in the winter, when faulty wiring and heating systems are taxed most. A fire last year burned out seven apartments. One man died.

Repeated complaints to the city housing authority about the fire hazards finally forced a visit to the building by a judge; he ordered 147 separate violations to be corrected. Two years later, not one of the repairs had been made.

Inside Miss Wender's three-room apartment itself, only the kitchen radiator works, so it is there she spends most of her time. The top of her thirty-year-old refrigerator is stacked with dishes and pots because water from the apartment above constantly leaks into the kitchen cabinets. Glass containers are suspended from wall hooks all over the small room; they are sealed with cork to frustrate mice and cockroaches.

The three entrances to the kitchen—from the outside hall, the bedroom and the bathroom—are covered with heavy blankets much of the year in a futile effort to stop the wind from blowing through the apartment. Similarly, every window is covered with something—pieces of plastic, cardboard, sheets—but the makeshift materials billow day and night with the wind.

Miss Wender is forced to use the burners on the gas stove for heat. "It's not only dangerous," she says, "but it costs a lot on my gas bills." Last winter, during a thirty-day period of below-freezing weather without heat, she almost set fire to her apartment. She heated a rock each night on the stove, wrapped it in rags and took it to bed with her. One night her hands were so cold she dropped the rock. The rags fell onto the stove and flamed. She was just barely able to put out the fire.

During those weeks, Miss Wender would lie in bed all day because of the cold. It was the only way she could keep warm. She rarely ate. She just lay in bed trembling and crying.

Sanitation is a serious problem as well. "I haven't

taken a real bath in years because there's no hot water," she says. "The closest I can come to being clean is with sponge baths." Sometimes there is no water at all, even cold water. For an entire month last summer, she had to carry water from an apartment across the street.

For ten months last year, her toilet was broken. She had to use plastic-lined containers for her wastes, seal them and put them in the toilet to dampen the odor as much as possible. "It got to the point where I was reluctant to eat because that meant I had to go to the bathroom." On occasion, the pipes backed up and raw sewage flooded the toilet and the sink.

Miss Wender has tried to escape these nightmarish living conditions. But there is no place for her to move except into low-cost city housing. And her application has been lost three times by the city housing department. Meanwhile, her landlord would like to force her out of the building; under a new city law, he then could raise the rent for the next tenant. Miss Wender pays $68 a month. A new tenant would pay an unbelievable $200 for the same apartment. "The landlord does things like claiming he hasn't received my rent checks," she says. "Lately he's been putting 'return to sender' on my phone bills before I even see them. I don't know how much more of this harassment I can take."

Neither her apartment nor the building is fit for use. Yet this old woman is unable to get out, even though her landlord tries to force her out. Meanwhile, her health, both physical and mental, is deteriorating. "There have been times when I think I approach madness," she says. "I have come close to suicide.

Because I can't even keep myself clean, I won't allow any friends to visit. I need to get out of here."

Rose Mary Wender has overcome a number of hardships in her life, including several major operations. But this one—housing—may finally destroy her. She is old. She is tired. She is depressed. At sixty-nine, she has nowhere to go and nowhere to seek help.

It is bad enough that anyone in a nation as prosperous as ours lives in such appalling surroundings. It is a national disgrace that thousands of our oldest citizens are forced to.

A woman in Chicago recently told me she spends all but $20 of her Social Security check—her total income—for house taxes and repairs and still can't pay her entire tax bill. She cuts back on heating oil, a dangerous thing to do with the kind of winters we have in that city. "I can't sell the house," she said. "It's all I have left."

A seventy-nine-year-old widow in a Baltimore suburb bought a home with her husband thirty-seven years ago. He died in 1956. She was able to work until 1965. Home and medical expenses take $1,200 of her $1,958 income each year. That leaves her $2.08 a day to live. She was just assessed $260 for sewer improvements.

But costs are not the whole story; sometimes official indifference is worse. "New York's Housing Maintenance Commission offered a dismal example of the sort of governmental insensitivity that makes growing old in a cold and thoughtless urban environment so needlessly unpleasant," *The New York Times* reported recently. "As thousands of low-income persons, sixty-two and older, rushed to meet the deadline for the filing of applications for partial exemption for rent increases, it became evident that few provisions had been made to prevent unnecessary hardships. ∿

"The forms are excessively complex. Delays in their delivery forced many applicants to wait in line, sometimes in heavy rain outside the district offices. In some instances, hard-to-negotiate stairs turned the mission into a cruel obstacle course. And the phone number on the brochure that had been mailed out was wrong. . . ."

There is much we can do to meet the elderly's housing needs. We should fully and aggressively begin to use our existing housing programs, programs that could lead to the construction of more than 1 million new units a year. A substantial portion of these units would go to the elderly poor—that is, if we go by the number of names on waiting lists for housing for the elderly, or if we provide money for projects now in advanced stages of planning. As I pointed out in an earlier chapter, to ask someone seventy, eighty or older to wait the three or four years required for a new apartment in so many of our cities is to ask quite a lot.

Allowances—direct cash payments to the elderly for housing purposes—might help some men and women find more suitable housing on the open market. This assumes that adequate, vacant housing exists within a given area, which is not usually the case today. Property tax relief for the elderly, joined with a program designed to help elderly homeowners keep their homes in good repair, also is a potential form of housing allowance for the 70 percent of the elderly who live in their own homes.

We need innovative and broad-based experiments in residences for the elderly, housing that would meet their special living needs and be close to the heart of any community—shops, churches, theaters.

Housing the elderly in unused college dormitories is one possibility that might be explored. Thousands of dorm rooms are empty because of declining enrollments. Why not use them to provide decent housing for the elderly and at the same time generate revenue for hard-pressed colleges and universities?

As a nation, we must consider all the housing requirements of older men and women: intelligent architectural design that will allow them to get about freely with canes, walkers, in wheelchairs; proximity to health-care facilities, meals and social activities; transportation to provide easy access to places they must go. Intelligent design would take into account that the elderly are individuals. Some may prefer to live in a multi-story apartment building; others would rather live in other types of housing—for example, low-rise apartments or townhouses. The elderly are extremely vulnerable to crime and their housing should provide adequate safeguards against this danger.

In 1971, I asked Congress to approve $75 million to build experimental housing and long-term-care facilities—ranging from intensive-care to convalescent units—on campus-like settings. This would reduce the amount of forced transfer from one facility to a totally foreign environment when failing health might demand it. Aging men and women are insecure enough, especially when their health deteriorates. They know that illness may force them to move to a different home, a different neighborhood. So they often are reluctant to complain of not feeling well.

One reason there is no cohesive national housing policy for the elderly is that would-be programs often are tangled in red tape and overlapping jurisdictions. No one person is ultimately responsible for dealing with the problem.

Several of us in Congress would like to establish the post of an assistant secretary of housing for the elderly in the Department of Housing and Urban Development. He or she should be sensitive to the special needs of the elderly and sufficiently high in the bureaucracy to get things done. Without such a high-level administrator concentrating on the housing (and related) needs of older Americans, it is unlikely that those needs can even begin to be met.

With or without heightened administrative focus on the housing plight of the elderly, not much can really change until bureaucratic procedures somehow are made more human. As noted earlier, a callous bureaucracy can often stand in the way of adequate medical care for the aged. The same holds true in housing.

To what extent should we encourage profit versus nonprofit sponsors of housing projects for the elderly? The nation established a program some years back that authorized direct loans from the federal government to nonprofit sponsors who would build housing for the elderly. Sponsors could borrow up to 100 percent of the project cost and repay the loan with 3 percent interest over fifty years. It was a successful and efficient effort. The sponsors, primarily church groups, were conscientious in looking after their elderly participants.

This effort was later supplemented by a new housing program. The federal government now underwrites only the difference between the 1 percent interest rate paid by the sponsor and the going market rate of commercial lenders—which in 1974 hovered around 9 percent.

It was never the intent of Congress to abandon the direct-loan program for the elderly. The new effort was intended to stimulate construction of rental housing by private groups for low-income individuals of all ages. Instead, it has gained a reputation for promoting get-rich-quick developers and shoddy construction. Unfortunately, it encourages low-rise, low-cost construction on inexpensive land, which removes elderly people from the transportation and shopping centers they need. Nonprofit sponsors who want to build now must go to commercial money lenders—who profit from high-interest loans—and compete with other applicants for loan money. The earlier program enjoyed property tax relief, which made lower rents possible. Its successor does not get that relief. In Spring 1974, the Senate approved legislation intended to tighten loopholes in this program considerably and to eliminate the opportunity for abuse. I have proposed legislation to reactivate the direct federal-loan program.

It is encouraging to note that a growing number of cities and states are creating varied forms of property tax relief for elderly home owners. Yet these men and women still pay proportionately more than twice as much in real estate taxes as the average younger family. Rising taxes and maintenance costs—up 39 percent and 33 percent respectively since 1968—are forcing retired home owners to move. For their comfort and quite possibly to forestall future housing problems, reasonable tax abatement for those over sixty-five is essential. In 1973 I co-authored a bill to help states provide property tax relief for low-income homeowners, primarily the elderly. If approved as now written, it would call for federal spending of $15 million the first year, $20 million the second and $25 million the third.

Whatever form it takes, we urgently need a rational and comprehensive policy on housing for the elderly. Without one, millions of older Americans will continue to be denied lives of independence, comfort and dignity.

9.

NURSING HOME OR WAREHOUSE

Stick a pin blindly into a list of all the nation's homes for the aged and you are apt to hit an atrocity. I have visited refugee camps in India and Pakistan where I found the refugees treated better than Americans in many of our nursing homes.

My friend Mary Adelaide Mendelson points out in her book, *Tender Loving Greed,* that no one has seen all or even most of the twenty-three thousand nursing homes in the United States. "Yet," she writes, "on the basis of my visits to more than 200 homes in various parts of the country, of testimony I have heard given to congressional hearings, and of my interviews with government regulators in many states, I have come across scant evidence or even hearsay of truly excellent facilities."

Unlike most U.S. hospitals,

which are nonprofit, 95 percent of American nursing homes are privately owned. Their chief purpose is to make money. They do make money—lots of it. In the course of some Senate hearings three years ago, one nursing home owner revealed that he had realized a $185,000 profit in one year on a $10,000 investment. (This extraordinary bonanza was more easily understood when we discovered that he was spending only 58 cents per day per patient on food.) You and I pay most nursing home profits by means of taxes routed through Medicaid and Medicare.

Carl Andersen is seventy-six and recently gave up the Iowa corn farm that his father started and Carl had worked full time since he left school at fourteen. "We used to get up at 4:30 every morning and go through until 6 or 7 at night. It was hard, but I liked working the land. I hated to give it up. But I like it here."

"Here" is the Bensenville Home in Bensenville, Illinois, where he now lives. It is a rare example of what a residential and nursing home can—and should—be. After his wife died, Mr. Andersen sold his small farm and tried to live with his daughter's family in downstate Illinois. That didn't succeed ("There's only so many bushels you can grow on an acre") and he moved to Bensenville. After years of working virtually alone all day, he likes the companionship in the home. He found he has a talent for furniture repair—chairs and other small items—which he practices in the home's shop. Mr. Andersen helps another widower, an eighty-three-year-old former shoe store manager, with a flower garden: hundreds of petunias, marigolds, poppies. "It's not quite the farm, but it's kind of fun." Mr. Andersen and a friend frequently walk about a quarter of a mile to the heart of downtown Bensenville for a beer and to see what's happening.

"Things are pretty good here. The food's good; not as good as my wife's but you can't be a perfectionist."

He has his own room—as does everyone at Bensenville—decorated with bright colors, curtains and good furniture. It could be a room in any private home.

The Bensenville Home, in a suburb of Chicago, was opened in 1895. It's a nonprofit, nonsectarian institution affiliated with the United Church of Christ. For the 4 or 5 percent of the aged who need this kind of attention, Bensenville proves it can be delivered with understanding, kindness and an appreciation of who they are and the unique needs they have.

The elderly, like most people, prefer to live in their own homes, no matter how fine a group-home might be. Many men and women who end up in an institution could remain at home if home care programs were available. "Too few communities provide the services to allow that," says Leroy H. Jones, executive director of Bensenville. "Beyond the personal benefit, it's far less expensive for a community to pay for these home services than to pay to keep a person in a nursing home.

"We're trying to make Bensenville not so much a custodial care institution as a 'therapeutic community' to meet outside needs," he says.

Bensenville delivers two meals—one a hot lunch—five days a week to nearby elderly men and women unable to cook for themselves. It is planning a day-care center so older people who need physical or occupational therapy, or just someone to talk with, can come during the day and go home each night.

Bensenville works equally hard for its residents. "We encourage everyone to participate in all our activities, to function within their capacities," says Mr. Jones. "We stress that this is their home even though it's group living. We want everyone to retain as much of his individuality as possible. There is room for self-expression and we expect it. We ask each resident to act as freely and in as individual a way as possible."

At another home, this one in an Eastern state, the atmosphere is radically different—and unfortunately more typical.

*"Stay away from him. He's a pain in the ass."

Henry Jefferd, eighty, is lonely and calls for aides for no real reason. They ignore him. Rarely do passing nurses or orderlies stop. When they do, they are curt, severe. It becomes a sad cycle: he wants attention; no one comes, or someone stops for only a moment; Henry becomes more upset and calls out again.

Eventually he is sedated. Henry has been receiving large doses of Thorazine, a powerful tranquilizer used primarily for neurotics. Yet no physician has ever called Henry neurotic.

When choice is possible, each Bensenville resident is asked to select his own room. He can choose his own color and the room is painted. He's en-

---

*All of the italicized portions in this chapter refer to the nursing home located in the Eastern state. They do not refer to Bensenville.

couraged to bring as much personal furniture as possible so his room will retain the flavor of his own home. He wears his own clothes if he is ambulatory. The interior of the buildings is painted in cheerful pastel colors. The decorations, furniture and window curtains are attempts to soften as much as possible the fact that Bensenville is an institution. Most of the staff wear street clothes.

The residents' clothes are ragged and stained. Residents rarely wear their own. Most come from a common pile. A woman may wear her own nightgown one night and someone else's the next. Clothes that belong to residents who died are put into a common pile. Each patient has a little cubbyhole, about 18 inches square, into which everything with his name on it is stuffed.

The staff often runs out of diapers and linens for patients who are incontinent. "When that happens," an aide says, "we make do with anything we have around. I've used rags or shower curtains."

Bensenville has an intensive physical therapy program, designed to cope with the wide range of problems that can afflict an elderly man or woman. During the past year, fifteen men and women were helped from a wheelchair existence—in several cases, they had been confined to wheelchairs for a long time before they came to Bensenville—to walkers, then to canes. Several of them have moved to the ambulatory floor and relative independence.

A variety of illnesses or injuries can harm bladder muscles. When that happens, a catheter—a tube inserted into the bladder and emptying into a bag—often is used. "The lack of bladder control, an obvious physical discomfort, is also an immense psychological

problem to the elderly," says Mrs. Maribyrd Econo-
mes, R.N. "It instills a feeling of helplessness and
increases the tendency of some to want to be left alone,
to withdraw. We emphasize strengthening bladder
muscles where possible to the point where the resident
again is in control. It's essential that each keep as much
self-esteem as possible."

*Dignity can die quickly. Everyone undresses and is
washed in front of everyone else. One man has been there a
month and has yet to take a bath. He doesn't want to be
washed. He wants to take a shower by himself. He's able to do
it, but no one will allow him to. Some residents fight hard to
keep the remnants of their dignity. One of the women recently
bit an orderly because the aide kept talking to her as one would
to a child.*

*To amuse themselves, staff members make up names for
the residents. One who gets confused is "Daffy" Decker.
Another, whose body is not as quick as it once was, becomes
"Myrtle the Turtle." The orderlies use these names in talking
to the residents. The patients object—in vain.*

Residents at Bensenville are encouraged to join as
many activities, within and outside the home, as they
are able. A small sewing room is aptly called the
"Stitch 'n' Chatter Shop." A number of clubs, ranging
from study of the Bible to pinochle, enjoy great
popularity. A 12-passenger station wagon takes residents shopping, to the library, on picnics and to
nearby athletic events.

*The home's chores are done by orderlies who work at
minimum wage. Their efforts reflect their pay. The turnover
among the orderlies is about one-third each week. They do
their job with distaste, obvious to even the most withdrawn of*

the elderly. They are untrained, a number of them drifters, often part-time, often callous.

Many of the patients, perhaps one out of five, wear restraints during the day and sometimes at night. Many of them wouldn't need restraints if the staff were willing to watch them. One orderly tied a woman resident into a lobby chair at seven one morning and left her there. The older woman called to another orderly passing by at 11 A.M. and pleaded to go to the bathroom. The second orderly freed her. The orderly who had tied the woman protested: "She's not allowed to go to the bathroom until 2 P.M."

An orderly walked into the men's ward shortly after coming on duty at 4 P.M. She found a resident whose hands were tied tightly with ordinary clothesline rope to the bedposts behind him. He had been tied there twelve hours earlier by the head nurse on the 11 P.M.-to-7 A.M. shift because he had taken a comb from the man in the adjoining bed. The orderly untied him. The elderly man's hands were terribly swollen; his wrists were scarred. The day nurse had refused to cut the man down because she was afraid of the night nurse who had tied him.

An incontinent woman had diarrhea. She wore a diaper, but she was changed so infrequently that the dried waste produced a severe itch. She scratched. When one of the orderlies came in, she saw the waste on the woman's hands and became very severe. "Don't you touch me," she commanded. When the resident tried to explain what had happened, the orderly yelled at her. The woman broke down and became hysterical.

One man is a loner. None of the staff talks to him and he talks to no one. He sits all day in a corner. "Don't go near him," says an orderly. "He's really obnoxious. He can't get along with anyone." Yet when a new orderly sat down and offered him a cigarette, they talked for half an hour. The others didn't seem to realize that he was only irritable because no one talked to him as an intelligent adult.

Counselors meet frequently with the elderly at Bensenville, helping them adjust to leaving their families and entering a new life in a group-home. They talk of loneliness, the loss of friends, the fear of having to make new friends in a new environment. They also talk candidly about death "because that's something preying on everyone's mind."

Residents rarely talk about death. Most understand this will be the last home they will have. If someone dies during the night, the body is taken out quietly. It's hard when a mortician comes during the day. No resident will speak of the person who died. Death surfaces only in emotional outbursts when an elderly man or woman will wish himself dead, shouting it out to anyone within hearing range.

Bensenville has a beauty shop that is especially crowded just before holidays as residents prepare to visit homes of children or friends. "We want to show the women who live here that they can remain attractive and well-groomed," the beautician says, "that here is another activity they can continue uninterrupted from their former lives."

Rather than spend the time to set the hair of women patients, some orderlies take the easy way out. They crop women's hair short.

Bensenville has a 1-to-3 ratio of staff to residents. Each shift is under the direction of a registered nurse. Everyone, from full-time medical and nursing staff through volunteers, receives periodic in-service training to help each respond better to the needs of the residents.

It's not uncommon to find a practical nurse acting as sole supervisor, assisted by a varying number of untrained orderlies.

An elderly man calls in vain for someone to help him during the night. He has tried to get assistance in the past by climbing out of bed and searching for an aide. He is crippled by arthritis. His legs are emaciated. He falls and can't get up. Now his two roommates call out. The elderly man had fallen four times before trying to summon help. In one attempt he cut his arm badly. The house doctor was called and put in twelve stitches. "He gave no anesthesia," the nurse assisting later reported.

The house doctor visits once a month. The last time he came, he checked all sixty residents in two hours.

Sometimes orderlies don't feed lunch to helpless patients. In one case, a woman who is not inclined to talk was not fed. Her tray lay there for nearly an hour. The janitor threw it out untouched. The woman didn't eat that day. No one noticed.

The men's ward often is not cleaned. A thin film of urine lay in the aisle running between the beds. The men, most of them walking barefoot, trail the urine back from the bathroom.

Many of the residents walk the floor at night. They're ignored by the staff. A woman, about seventy-five, calls out. Orderlies chatting at the end of the corridor wait fifteen minutes before one breaks off from the group and goes to her. She gives the woman a sleeping pill. The woman still cannot sleep and calls again. No one responds.

Three electrical fires have occurred in recent years. On

one recent night shift, only one nurse and three orderlies came to work. They are supposed to be stationed throughout the home, including the second floor ward, to watch the patients. They all gather instead in a corner downstairs and chat. If a fire started . . .? "I'd get as many patients out as I could," says the nurse. "All of them? Impossible."

Bensenville's fees range from $390 to $685 a month, depending on the services needed. It runs at a significant deficit.

The fees at the Eastern home range from $540 to $620 a month. Its owner bought two more nursing homes within a year after he purchased this one.

We Americans allow a deeply disturbing situation to continue with regard to nursing homes. Our public funds provide most of their support, $2 billion each year. Yet regulation of nursing homes is so fragmented among local, county, state and federal agencies that it amounts to almost no regulation at all. For example, the state agency supervisor who evaluates and licenses the Eastern nursing home discussed above had no record of the three fires. Had she ever been in that home? "Years ago; I was in it once."

The General Accounting Office, the auditing arm of Congress, recently examined ninety nursing homes that were certified to provide skilled nursing care to Medicaid patients. Serious deficiencies were found in more than half the institutions. Most did not meet skilled-nurse standards. Forty-seven failed to comply with the regulation that a physician examine each resident at least once a month.

Close to half of the homes had inadequate fire protection or warning devices. Stories of disastrous fires in nursing homes are familiar to us all. But these tragedies seem to have little lasting impact. I asked one woman in a wheelchair in a Chicago nursing home what she would do if a fire broke out. Her reply: "Trust in God, I guess." That home held no fire drills, a violation of state law. In May 1972, the Carver Convalescent Home in Springfield, Illinois, occupied by low-income blacks on welfare, was destroyed by a fire that began during the night. Ten people died.

Mrs. Percy and I visited the home and talked with some of the residents. We learned that there was no warning system. There had been no fire drill within the memory of any resident. There was no standby emergency lighting, so most of the residents had no light as they tried to grope their way out. The second-floor emergency exit was a stairway so narrow that firemen on the ground floor had to wait until patients descended before they could climb up.

Shortly after the Carver fire, my colleague Senator Ted Moss introduced the Nursing Home Fire Safety Act, which I co-sponsored. The bill became law. The Department of Housing and Urban Development authorized loans to nursing homes for the purchase and installation of fire-safety equipment. The Department of Health, Education, and Welfare issued firmer regulations for the inspection and certification of nursing homes.

At the Eastern nursing home discussed earlier, men and women offering absolutely no credentials are hired on the spot and put to work providing the most intimate kind of patient care. They receive no instruction, no preparation.

This is not an isolated instance. Fewer than half

of this country's twenty-three thousand nursing homes offer skilled nursing care. In a Chicago home, an investigative reporter was taken on as a handyman and seventy-two hours later was appointed chief administrator. At the same home, a derelict was hired and in less than twenty-four hours was told to dispense medications, including narcotics. In another home, an aide and a janitor were instructed to dispense medicine. "I'm not really too sure who gets what medication, but I'll do my best," the aide told the janitor. "Oh, this lady is out of medicine, but I'll just borrow some from this lady."

The fact is, training programs for health personnel in nursing homes were virtually nonexistent until very recently. In part, lack of training may be rooted in the widely held belief that, if a person requires nursing home care, there can be little hope of his ever becoming self-sufficient and independent. For many this is probably true.

But the noted psychiatrist, Dr. Karl Menninger, told me of eighty-eight aged men and women who had been diagnosed as helplessly senile and psychotic and placed in a geriatric ward at Topeka State Hospital, Kansas. They had been there for ten years or more when a young, new doctor arrived with a new staff. By providing music, birds and plants, and by initiating a social program, they totally transformed a cheerless atmosphere. And they achieved significant results. One patient was discharged within three weeks. A year later, only nine patients were bedridden; only six were incontinent. During that first year, twelve more returned to live with their families. Six left to live alone.

Unfortunately, such stories are the exception rather than the rule. In lieu of personalized care, all too often nursing homes use tranquilizers to keep residents sedated. During an investigation in Illinois, by using the Senate power to subpoena records, we learned that drugs designed to treat the central nervous system, which includes tranquilizers, represent about 35 percent of the total amount spent for all nursing home drugs. Money used for just two tranquilizers, Thorazine and the closely related Mellaril, exceeded $100,-000 in four months in Illinois alone. One can only guess what the national expense for those two drugs over a year would be. It's an effective if cynical way to put residents in a position where they will not complain, not ask for too much service; then service can be reduced still further to increase profits.

In recent years, we have made some progress in the effort to upgrade nursing homes. Senate investigative hearings which I chaired with Senator Moss led to tougher federal standards and enforcement procedures for all such homes. Many of us in Congress contributed to an omnibus reform bill which passed in late 1972. And President Nixon responded to the problem by launching an eight-point nursing home improvement program by executive order. While all these actions have had a positive effect, far too many nursing homes remain substandard. What else should we do about conditions in our long-term care facilities?

Our primary goal, of course, should be to keep our elderly out of these institutions as long as possible. Wherever feasible, we should assist the older person to remain in his or her own home. Home-health services, such as home-delivered meals and other home-maintenance aids, are valuable means to this end. Another approach is to provide incentives to families to keep older persons at home. For instance, direct cash payments, or special tax deductions for families who are supporting aged relatives in their homes might be implemented.

Inevitably, some elderly men and women will find long-term-care facilities more appropriate for their needs. What we must do is to make sure that the high quality of care that characterizes homes like Bensenville becomes the standard rather than the exception.

We should structure our reimbursement system in such a way that nursing homes have an incentive to assist the patient to live a full and meaningful life. For example, we can require rehabilitative services in long-term-care facilities and provide 100 percent federal reimbursement for every resident who benefits from them.

We can build on past advances in a number of different ways. First, we can vigorously enforce existing nursing care regulations. I believe the quality of care would dramatically improve if we would but enforce present requirements for skilled nursing facilities and intermediate care facilities.

Until now, we have been satisfied with substantial compliance or we have winked at violations because we have been afraid that enforcing regulations would mean closing homes. One answer to this problem is to provide low-interest, government-insured loans to those nursing homes that can be brought up to standard in a reasonable length of time. Other facilities, I believe, should be closed.

Secondly, we should continue full federal reimbursement for the training and compensation of state nursing home inspectors, and we should make it mandatory for all nonprofessional employees of long-term institutions to receive pre-service and in-service training.

Finally, we should act in a number of ways to make nursing homes more accessible to the community they serve and, in that manner, make them more accountable to the community. We need to establish a nursing home ombudsman in every state. I would like to see HEW publish and widely distribute inspection reports written in easily understood terms. I can think of no quicker way to gain full compliance with standards of quality care than by making all deficiencies a matter of public record. If we can publish the names of restaurants and food stores that are cited for violation of public health codes, then surely we should go even further when the care of elderly human beings in nursing homes is at stake.

Young men and women often tell me they want to become involved in the serious social problems of our time. They want to help eliminate poverty and clean up the environment. In many cases, they're willing to exert extraordinary effort to help solve these problems. Yet they frequently discover the problems are so large they defy even partial solutions—at least on an individual basis.

There is one problem to which I believe young

people might direct more of their attention, the problem of overwhelming loneliness and despair among our aged citizens. Young people seem particularly well-suited to solve this problem, and it is one where small efforts can have great impact.

Two years ago, I wrote to many Illinois high school students urging them to devote some of their time and their talents to the problems of the elderly. At the same time, I wrote to nursing home administrators, suggesting, "The very young and the very old get along well with each other. In all the talk these days of a 'generation gap,' those two age groups communicate remarkably well.

"The establishment of volunteer youth corps in nursing homes throughout the state might help immeasurably to improve the spirits of chronically ill and lonely nursing home residents."

Many of the high school youngsters and a number of the nursing homes responded to these suggestions. Volunteer programs began in a variety of ways that still continue. I learned that residents of the nursing homes were dressing up on the days they knew the young people were to come. They invited their visitors to stay for a cup of tea. They started calling these comparative strangers "my grandchildren" and a number of the student volunteers responded with "Grandma" and "Grandpa."

At one nursing home on the south side of Chicago, a group of high school students continue to come into the home on a daily basis to work voluntarily as "junior aides." They run errands and perform a variety of services for the elderly patients. But, more important, their presence changes the entire atmosphere from one of depression and stultifying inactivity to one of cheer. They provide a measure of laughter, spontaneity and gayety. They have the energy to create many of their own projects. Most significantly, they come with a willingness to talk with the residents. They bring a piece of the outside world into an otherwise isolated and lonely atmosphere.

While the students' willingness to work with older people is wonderfully gratifying, it seems terribly sad that relatives of nursing home residents do not themselves do more to relieve the loneliness of their elders.

One reason for the poor quality of life in so many nursing homes may have to do with the stigma—and guilt—which often is attached to committing an elderly parent to such an institution. Many people apparently find it easier to stay away than to be regularly reminded of the dismal living conditions to which their parent or grandparent is probably being subjected. The administrator of one large nursing home told me that 200 of his patients had never had a single visitor.

Given adequate public support, government can help to improve conditions in our institutions for the elderly. But there is not a great deal government can do about the heart and the human spirit.

10.

SENIOR POWER: SEEKING A PLACE AT THE TABLE

Once north of Syracuse, New York, the cities fall away and the countryside is reclaimed. Towns of 2,000 and 1,500 appear—and disappear—quickly. Snuggled between the St. Lawrence Seaway and Adirondack Mountains is the community of Watertown.

Watertown was founded in 1800 and was made the county seat of Jefferson County five years later. Its population slowly grew until it reached 34,000 in 1944. But, in the years since, industries contracted or left altogether, and today summer tourism is its main attraction, thanks to nearby Lake Ontario and the Seaway.

Leaving with most of the industries over the years were many young men and women of the area. There is today a surplus of people under fourteen and over sixty. Of the older group, one of four lives below the poverty line, a bit worse than the national average. While it is hard to be old and poor in the city, to be old and poor in a rural area often is worse. There are two reasons for this: public transportation does not exist and physicians usually cluster in the local metropolis—in this case Watertown.

Drawn together by their common problems, in the late 1960s elderly men and women in a number of the county's communities began to organize. The 1971 White House Conference on Aging helped promote the concept that a union of twenty-seven separate community groups of elderly men and women might force faster solutions to problems they all shared.

By 1972, there was a countywide steering committee, the Senior Action Council of Jefferson County—SAC. (The first name proposed for the group—the Jefferson County Council on the Aging—was rejected when too many members objected to the word "aging.") One ticklish problem was persuading still-active farmers, sixty-five and older, that they should join. "Age has no relevance to them," says one organizer. "We had a hell of a time convincing them they're old people and should join an 'old people's' organization; they still work a fourteen-hour day."

The new amalgam of the elderly men and women of Jefferson County into one united body meant that the largest minority in the county could begin to speak with one voice. They wasted little time.

Of the county's ninety-one physicians, only twenty-one work in rural areas. Because the county is poor and rural, many medical practices end when physicians die or retire. The first priority of the Senior Action Council, therefore, was an obvious one: establish free medical screening clinics throughout the county where the elderly could receive regular health examinations.

Mercy Hospital in Watertown—the county's largest—was asked to provide the medical skills. The hospital imposed a condition of sincerity: SAC had to raise the money itself for a five-clinic experiment. It took the council less than five months to collect $9,350 from private sources. By May 1973, the free clinics were operating. They handled 1,200 patient-visits in their first seven months, an excellent beginning considering that none of the five towns housing a clinic had more than 2,000 residents.

Because the clinics are free and near, they make preventive medicine a reality for the first time in the lives of most of Jefferson County's elderly. Virtually all of the men and women who now visit the clinics previously would not or could not have taken the necessary day off to learn if they had a medical problem. Many could not afford the diagnostic tests if they had to go to a doctor or a hospital.

The clinics only screen and refer. Anyone who needs treatment is sent to his or her own physician or to a county public health nurse. Clinic personnel follow through, with visits to a person's home if necessary, to be sure referral is not ignored.

The special focus of the clinics is prevention of strokes and heart attacks—major problems for the elderly. Thirty-three percent of the men and women tested in the first seven months were found to have high blood pressure or to be approaching it. High blood pressure can be a precursor of heart problems and strokes. The clinics provide a range of tests. Each person who attends also receives individual "health education" counsel, information related to what that person must do to stay as healthy as possible.

SAC plans to open seven more clinics with the aid of a federal grant. The eventual goal is a comprehensive home health system. SAC is pressuring the County Board of Supervisors to increase the number of county-employed public health nurses and home health aides; by providing increased home services, elderly people who are ill can remain in their homes—and thus out of institutions—as long as possible.

The clinics have had a variety of positive effects on the communities they serve. "Because we had the clinics in operation," says Sister Edna, an administrator of Watertown's Mercy Hospital, "we were able to secure a $4,000 grant from the American Cancer Society for Pap tests. The fact that the clinics already existed proved our willingness to do the work we say we will do.

"This has been an underlying thought about the clinics since the start. We believed if we could build the foundation ourselves, it would be easier to get outside aid. The federal grant that will allow us to expand the clinics also will purchase a mobile unit to bring tests to people's homes. Because uterine cancer is most prevalent in women over fifty-five, the mobile unit's ability to do the Pap smear, for example, fits right into the health priority of SAC.

"We envision a number of things based on those first five clinics. We'll be able slowly to add tests, employees and service. We would like to integrate the activities of our men and women over sixty-five with the hospital's nursing home, the Madonna Home. We dream of the day when the nursing home will be a day center for the county's aging, one that will provide services by day and allow them to live at home. Right now, we're working on plans for a 'geriatric swimming pool' on the grounds of the nursing home for use by the elderly. We could dream of none of this if it hadn't been for SAC and the screening clinics."

Nutritional considerations were involved in SAC's initial decision to concentrate on better health care; four hot lunch programs already have begun with the aid of federal money.

But more than improved health emanated from the clinics. The men and women who led the drive for the clinics discovered in their success that indeed there is strength in numbers. SAC, in other words, is learning about political muscle and is beginning to use it. Awareness of power and political clout comes slowly to a group unfamiliar with its uses. But it has come to Watertown. "We no longer will be satisfied with second-class citizenship," says Carl Eberhart, sixty-eight, a SAC leader. "We can accomplish things. We'll not be a disruptive force. But we will let our thoughts be known.

"I think our group in Clayton [one of the Jefferson County communities that make up SAC] was responsible for defeating an outrageous school referendum here," he explains. "The referendum included an Olympic-size pool and a luxurious gymnasium. Every classroom was larger than state specification. After the issue was defeated, the school board realized we were a force to be reckoned with. They asked permission to speak at one of our meetings. We told them how we felt about the school plans. Eventually, $3 million was cut and the referendum passed."

SAC has a priority list. "We're going to take one step at a time and not be satisfied until each objective is reached," says Mr. Eberhart. "We want a tax abatement program for men and women over sixty-five at both the county and community levels." Watertown already allows a 50 percent reduction in city taxes to elderly residents who earn under $3,000. "We have not yet approached the county, but we will," Mr. Eberhart adds. "I'm going to use a soft approach. I hope I don't have to organize a lot of seniors to come out with me. But if the board isn't receptive, it's going to have a crowd on its hands. I have no doubt that we could bring 500 to 600 members to a meeting of a community or county governing body if a matter important to us was on the agenda."

"SAC will grow in many directions," said adviser Dick Charles of the Jefferson County Community Action Planning Council, an agency of the federal Office of Economic Opportunity. "Its third priority after health and tax abatement is transportation. There is none in the county. When taxi drivers went on strike recently, it was virtually a crisis. SAC used its influence in getting that strike settled. They are going to see now what they can do about some kind of bus system.

"SAC is going to force all the many legislative and agency groups that deal with the aging on community, county and state levels to work with it. SAC will prove that the elderly cannot be stereotyped, that they are a force to be reckoned with, that people in elected and appointed jobs have an obligation to them. They're moving fast—faster than many men and women half their age."

Only in the past few years have elderly men and women begun to realize what they can achieve together through public relations and in the voting booth. Although they comprise but 10 percent of our population, they accounted for 17 percent of the vote in the last national election, far more proportionately than any other age group in the nation. Already, some of their accomplishments are impressive.

The Chicago Area Council of Senior Citizens Organizations, which represents 15,000 members, last year probed the subject of nursing homes. Thanks in part to their investigation, fifteen homes were forced to close. When a Medicaid cutback was threatened in New York State, thousands of elderly protested. There were no cuts. In New York City, about 1,000 elderly men and women, some in wheelchairs, demonstrated at City Hall to urge tax abatement for certain landlords of apartments occupied by elderly tenants with rent exemptions. The abatement was provided.

In Pontiac, Michigan, elderly men and women physically blocked traffic on streets where they believed hazards existed. Traffic lights were quickly installed. In San Francisco, a group of men and women over sixty-five threatened to walk all the way to Sacramento, the state capital, if a bill increasing old-age assistance was not signed by the governor. It was signed. The 245,000-member Council of Retired Workers of the United Auto Workers, which has helped enrich the lives of thousands of retirees sent thousands of members in Detroit, Cleveland, New York and other cities during the 1970 strike against General Motors to demand additional benefits for retired men and women. The auto maker provided more pension money and better insurance benefits in the new contract. Henry A. Sherman, a seventy-four-year-old retired army colonel and a delegate to the 1971 White House Conference on Aging, organized a political action group of the elderly in Houston and soon won a victory: reduced fare on city buses. "Now come the gas, telephone and electric companies and then the stores," Mr. Sherman vowed.

"Our decade is witnessing the rise of a very different generation of elders," says Margaret Kuhn, founder of the Gray Panthers, another political action group of the elderly. "We live longer. We're more vigorous physically. We're better educated and more articulate. And we are becoming aware how our society puts us down. I would hope that the revolution of the elders, contrary to other revolutions, would be a unifying force in a society that is fear-ridden and divided. Age is the great universalizer. We're all growing old, every one of us. The problem is how to deal with growing old. The Gray Panthers and other like-minded groups are muscling in on society. We'll do it with militancy, demonstrations, anything to get a place at the table."

Ed Kiefer, seventy-three-year-old Republican chairman of Pinellas County in Florida, has declared that every statewide candidate there "must take a stand on matters of vital interest to the older people or lose at the polls. There is no question that the seniors, voting in a bloc, would be able to elect or defeat any candidate on the statewide ballot."

Major Roy Nordheimer, eighty-three, an adviser to the Chicago Area Council of Senior Citizens Organizations, warns that "there is an increasing feeling among our people that, if we can't get what we need, we'll have to be more drastic."

Senior power is just beginning to coalesce. Retired men and women generally not only have valuable experience, but sufficient time and community contacts, fewer family obligations, and a potential for free thinking unhampered by career ambitions. As fragmented groups of the movement become better coordinated, and as they learn to work more closely with non-elderly who share their goals, their influence will continue to grow.

Senior power is an important new force in America. Most men and women over sixty-five find it hard at first to do what others in our country have done for decades: stand up and demand attention to issues they consider important. But they are learning. They are learning quickly to touch the pressure points of our society.

11.

TO BELONG TO LIFE

No number of surveys, studies or
hearings will put an end to the
misery of so many of our aged until
we change our basic attitude toward
them. The appalling conditions that
confront millions of elderly
Americans—substandard housing,
inadequate health care, and deficient
diets—are a harsh commentary on
our national indifference toward the
aged. But psychologically perhaps
the most devastating condition of all
is their loneliness.

On a visit to a Chicago nursing
home in the summer of 1974, I met
an elderly woman who poignantly
underscored the value of human
contact. She had spent twenty-seven
years in nursing homes. During all
those years she had received only
thirty letters, and she had them
wrapped in what she

called "my precious bundle." She kept it under her pillow.

"When people are isolated from their normal environments, no longer see their friends and loved ones, no longer contribute to society, they regress and die," says a North Carolina family physician. "I have seen old people in a reasonably healthy condition who, when put away in the isolation of custodial-care facilities, lost total interest in life. They refused to communicate, refused to eat, became totally bedridden, wasted away and died. This is a disease process called 'isolation' and should be so designated on the death certificate." Says a seventy-two-year-old man in a barren Chicago nursing home, "I do not belong to life."

"The major psychological state we are treating in our elderly people is depression," says one psychiatrist. "Depression is almost universal in older people." Depression usually begins when elderly men and women, after years of independence, find themselves ignored by a society that no longer has time for them. Withdrawal and loneliness are the inevitable results. A physician in Illinois told me of the many visits he receives from elderly patients in whom he can find no tangible medical problems. The doctor finally asked one man what exactly was troubling him. The patient answered with unexpected frankness: "To tell the truth, doctor, I guess I came here because you're the only one I have to talk with."

Why are the elderly so lonely? Where are their relatives? One gerontologist explains, "Out of feelings of guilt and regret, children, grandchildren and other relatives often 'distance' themselves from the elderly.

It's a subtle rejection and the victim reacts defensively, by dwelling on the past, by withdrawing and, occasionally, striking out."

Loneliness complicates other problems. Often, it adversely affects the motivation of older people to eat and to exercise properly. "You'll see people afraid to take a bath because they fear that if they fall in the tub, no one would know about it," says Mrs. Sadelle Greenblatt of Chicago's Council for Community Services. "So they don't bathe. Or people who have kept their homes immaculate no longer have the strength to do it. So they'll shut themselves inside their apartments and refuse to let anyone see that their near-perfect house isn't as clean as it once was."

The American Friends Service Committee reports, "Many old people spend hour upon hour in public places just to fill their empty days. The waiting rooms of bus terminals and train stations are full of them."

The empty days and empty lives take a brutal toll. The rate of suicide among men and women over sixty-five is 20 percent higher than the national average for all age groups. "Depressed elderly men and women are often potentially suicidal," says Dr. Francis J. Braceland of the Institute of Living in Hartford, Connecticut. "They play a kind of Russian roulette in which the patient is prepared to gamble the chance of losing his life against the possibility that things will improve if he survives. The possibility of suicide must always be kept in mind, especially in depressed men or women who see no reason for going on and who have convinced themselves that their departure would make life easier for others."

"Old people need a modicum of attention and a reasonably generous dose of being listened to. Evidence of affection toward them is better than drugs. They need to know they are still regarded as being in the land of the living."

Honor and respect for those who have preceded us need not spring only from altruistic motives. We have much to learn from the elderly if we listen. As their own historians, they can be prophets among us. They can assess our culture with the perspective provided by years of experience, and they can prepare us for the day when we will be the senior generation. If we dismiss the ideas of those who have come before us, we invite our own failure. "You take all the experience and judgment of men over fifty out of the world," observed Henry Ford, "and there wouldn't be enough left to run it."

Today's elderly Americans are a pioneer generation; they are the first in history to experience a long and early retirement. As it now stands, however, their situation is a grim harbinger of our own futures. If older men and women today don't have adequate housing, incomes, diets, health care and transportation facilities, what miracle will bring those things *to us* when we reach retirement age? Because we probably will enjoy longer lives than our parents, there will be more of us making demands on limited resources.

If compassion or self-interest does not move us as a nation to deal with the isolation of our elderly, perhaps economics will. "Studies show a correlation between isolation and poor health which in turn lead to admission to long-term facilities—often at great expense to the public," says former HEW Secretary

Elliot Richardson. "If we were willing to do a little more to overcome the barriers of isolation, we would not only contribute to the happiness and productivity of the older individual, but at the same time we would avoid heavy, long-term costs."

It is a sad irony that as we achieve advancements in medicine and technology that make it possible to prolong life, we also are pushing older persons out of the mainstream of American society. We limit their options in employment, recreation and education.

The U.S. Public Health Service reports that recent advances in scientific knowledge and techniques now make it possible to address many of the key questions about aging. Some of these concern the role of immunity in aging, the effect of age on the cells, and the effect of nutrition and environment on aging in humans.

Yet the federal government severely cut research funds in 1974. "The only programs in this country that are developing knowledge and training personnel to meet the problems of the elderly were drastically affected by this cut," the Senate Special Committee on Aging reported. "A single breakthrough in the delay of senile dementia might save over $1 billion a year, in addition to immeasurable human anguish," says Dr. Marrott Sinex, biochemist at Boston University's School of Medicine. "We ought to be able to at least partially solve this problem through research."

Less than 15 cents per American will be spent for investigation into the biological origins of aging during 1974. The Department of Defense will spend an estimated $50 per person during the same period. "There is no single feature of the human situation that

produces more universal loss and suffering, both physical and mental, than the process of aging," says Dr.
Bernard L. Strehler, professor of biology at the University of Southern California. "Because research bud-
gets have been castrated during the last two adminis-
trations, the needed resources are not being supplied
by the only source suited to supply them—the federal
government."

The fact is that if we hope to implement many of
the programs and proposals touched upon in these
pages, it will take many millions of dollars which
ultimately will come out of the pockets of American
taxpayers.

Those of us serving in government can make
endless speeches on the plight of the elderly. We can
make proposals and even write books. But until a
significant number of Americans are willing and deter-
mined to pay for what needs to be done, the elderly
will continue to exist on the fringes of our society. Too
often they will remain hungry and without adequate
medical care, poor and ill-housed, ignored and alone.

Today, 5 million Americans sixty-five and
over—one out of every four—are destined to die alone
and unattended; in many cases, their deaths will go
unnoticed for days or even weeks. By itself, that
statistic is a searing commentary on our attitude
toward the aged. Small wonder that so many of them
feel terribly cynical, their cynicism reflected in the
bitter parody of a bedtime prayer overheard in a
nursing home: "Now I lay me down to sleep / I pray
the Lord my soul to keep/If I should die before I wake/
Who the hell would care?"

Somehow, we have to care more than we do now about the elderly dispossessed in America.

How deeply do we care when millions of our parents and grandparents die indirectly because of malnutrition or infectious diseases, both largely preventable and treatable?

How deeply do we care when as a nation we spend $14 million to build a single fighter airplane and the same amount for research into problems of aging?

How deeply can we care when we maintain demeaning, dehumanizing nursing homes on local, county and state levels for 1 million older Americans?

How deeply do we care when we permit highly qualified elderly workers to be forced out of jobs which they need?

Many of us in government, as in other fields, will continue to fight for the rights and the needs of the elderly in this country. We are fully committed to that struggle. But we will neither secure those rights nor fulfill those needs without much broader and deeper support from vast numbers of our fellow citizens. Without that support, the pursuit of happiness will continue to come to an abrupt halt for millions at age sixty-five.

In many ways, the American experiment has been an extraordinary social, economic and political success. But until we enable our older citizens to live out their lives with a much greater degree of dignity than is now commonly available to them, the experiment will fall short of its potential and its promise.

ACTION
RESOURCE GUIDE

ACTION RESOURCE GUIDE

Introduction

Each of us, at one time or another, has needed information and not known where to find it. The purpose of this Action Resource Guide is to provide specific, practical information for the elderly—to tell you what benefits you are entitled to, to advise you where to go for help in solving problems, to point out what opportunities exist for people over sixty-five.

Your questions may range from the easy-to-answer ("Am I eligible for Social Security benefits?") to the qualitative ("How can I tell a good nursing home from a bad one?") to the highly individualized puzzler that will have to be researched ("Can I get free medical attention for a shrapnel wound I received in the Solomon Islands in World War II?"). You may not find all the answers here, but I *will* tell you where to go for additional information.

In many instances, I have included addresses—and sometimes even telephone numbers—of governmental agencies and nongovernmental groups throughout the nation that can assist you.

1.

FINANCIAL BENEFITS

SOCIAL SECURITY

Social Security is a program of social insurance administered by the Social Security Administration of the U.S. Department of Health, Education, and Welfare. It is available to *almost every retired American* and many disabled people, as well as their dependents and survivors.

During your working years, money is deducted from each paycheck and deposited in a trust fund. When you retire, you receive monthly Social Security checks based on your former earnings, whether you worked for others or were self-employed.

If you plan to retire in the next two or three months, *apply now* for Social Security benefits at the nearest Social Security office. If you are already retired, disabled, or the dependent of someone who is retired or disabled, or if you are the survivor of someone who has worked, and you are *not* receiving Social Security checks, you may be entitled to receive monthly benefits. *No one can receive Social Security benefits without filing an application.*

When you visit the Social Security office to apply for benefits, *bring the following*:

(1) Your Social Security card or a record of your Social Security number;
(2) Your birth certificate or other proof of age;
(3) Your last W-2 Form wage and tax statement, or a copy of your last federal income tax return if you are self-employed.

If you cannot locate any of these items, ask someone at the Social Security office what other documents can be used to fulfill proof of identification and earnings requirements. *Don't delay applying for benefits just because you think you don't have the proper documents.*

Even if you *think* you are not eligible for Social Security benefits, it is a good idea to check with the local Social Security office. You may discover that you are eligible after all to receive monthly benefits.

The basic questions and answers that follow may help you understand more fully how Social Security works.

Q. I will be sixty-five in a couple of months, but I plan to continue working. Should I apply for Social Security benefits now?

A. Yes. That way you will ensure your eligibility for Medicare benefits (see p. 153) when you become sixty-five. You can receive Medicare even if you are working. When you do retire, let the Social Security office know and your monthly checks will start immediately.

Q. Can I retire at sixty-two and still get Social Security benefits?

A. You can retire at any time after your sixty-second birthday and begin to receive benefits. *However, your checks will be smaller than if you wait to retire at age sixty-five. You will have to wait until you are sixty-five* to receive Medicare coverage. *Before* you decide to retire early, check with your local Social Security office to learn exactly how much your check will be if you decide to retire at age sixty-two or sixty-four. (You can also consult the pamphlet *Estimating Your Social Security Retirement Check*, available at the office.) You may find that it is worth waiting the additional two or three years to retire so that you will receive larger monthly retirement checks.

Q. Six weeks have passed since I filed my application for Social Security and I haven't received a check. What should I do?

A. Let your Social Security office know this right away. Everything possible will be done to speed up the process. If your application is rejected for some reason, you have the right to ask for reconsideration. If it is turned down a second time, you may ask for a review by a hearing examiner. There is no charge for these services.

Q. I am receiving monthly Social Security checks. Will I lose them if I take a job?

A. As of 1974, you can earn up to $2,400 a year without having any part of your Social Security check withheld. Above $2,400, $1 is withheld for each $2 that you earn. *However, if you are seventy-two or older, you can earn as much money as you want and still receive your full check.* Your Social Security check will not be reduced because of income from savings, investments, pensions or insurance, whatever your age.

Q. I am not planning to retire for a few more years. Is there anything I should do now to prepare for retirement?

A. There are five items you should collect and put in a safe place: your Social Security card or a record of your Social Security number; copies of your annual W-2 wage and tax statements that record your earnings; your marriage certificate (if you are married); your birth certificate; and the birth certificates of other members of your immediate family (husband, wife or children). Be sure to tell a responsible member of your family where those papers are, so if you should die or become incapacitated your survivors or dependents will be able to apply for Social Security benefits.

Q. Are self-employed persons eligible for Social Security benefits?

A. Yes. Self-employed individuals also contribute to the Social Security trust fund and are eligible for both Social Security checks and Medicare. For details, ask your Social Security office to send you a copy of its pamphlet written for self-employed people. There are additional special pamphlets for self-employed farmers.

Q. I am disabled, but I don't know if my disability is permanent. Can I receive Social Security benefits?

A. If it appears that your disability will last a year or more, you should apply for benefits immediately. There is a waiting period of five months before you will get your first check. Ask your nearest Social Security office for a copy of *If You Become Disabled* for a full explanation of payments to the disabled.

Q. If I receive disability checks and then return to work, will the checks stop?

A. The law allows for a nine-month trial work period after resuming work to see whether you can manage working again. During that time, the checks will continue. If you find after nine months that you cannot keep working, you will continue to receive monthly disability checks. If you can do substantial work after the nine-month period, you will receive checks for three more months before they stop. If you are receiving Workmen's Compensation for the disability, your Social Security checks *may* be reduced.

If you are disabled but can perform some work, your state's vocational rehabilitation agency may be able to help you find a suitable job. Ask at your Social Security office about such assistance.

Q. What is the definition of "disabled"?

A. According to law, disabled means you have a physical or mental condition that prevents you from doing substantial gainful work for at least one year. Your age, education, training and experience may be taken into consideration in deciding whether or not you are disabled.

Q. Can I get Medicare benefits if I am disabled but under sixty-five?

A. Medicare protection is available to any disabled person under sixty-five who has been entitled to Social Security disability benefits for at least two years. Check with your Social Security office to find out if you are eligible to apply for Medicare.

Q. What payments can be made to dependents of disabled, retired or deceased Social Security recipients?

A. If you are disabled, payments can be made:

(1) to your unmarried children under age eighteen;
(2) to your unmarried children eighteen to twenty-two if they are attending school full time;
(3) to your unmarried children eighteen or older who were themselves disabled before reaching age twenty-two and continue to be disabled;
(4) to your wife if she cares for a child who is getting benefits because the child is under eighteen or became disabled before age twenty-two;
(5) to your wife if she is sixty-two or older;
(6) to your dependent husband if he is sixty-two or older.

If you are not disabled but you retire or die,

your children will receive payments until the age of eighteen, or until they are twenty-two if they remain unmarried and in school full time. Wives and dependent husbands and widows and dependent widowers also will receive Social Security checks when the person who is eligible for Social Security payments retires or dies.

Q. What should I do if a family member dies?

A. Go to the nearest Social Security office with the Social Security number of the person who died and the death certificate. If you want to apply for survivor's benefits, bring a marriage certificate and birth certificates of all children under twenty-two. Even if you have no other claim, apply for the lump-sum death payment. (If you are not sure whether the person who died was eligible for Social Security benefits, check with the Social Security office anyway. You may learn that the person was eligible and that you can file for death or survivor's benefits.)

To locate the Social Security office nearest your home, consult your telephone directory under U.S. government, state, or city government listings. Or ask the directory assistance (information) operator for help. If you do not have a telephone, your post office will have the address. If there is no Social Security office in your area, call the office in the nearest city *collect.* (Employees will accept collect calls from areas that don't have Social Security offices.)

In all likelihood, if your community has no Social Security office, a field representative visits on a regular basis. You can find out when he comes by asking at the post office. If you are in a hospital, a nursing home, or cannot leave your home and have a problem that requires personal contact with a Social Security representative, one will make an appointment to visit you.

SUPPLEMENTAL SECURITY INCOME
Supplemental Security Income, a program administered by the Social Security Administration, currently guarantees a total monthly cash income of $146 to an individual and $219 to a couple.
You are eligible for Supplementary Security Income if:

(1) you are sixty-five or older;
(2) you have a monthly income of less than $140 (individual) or $210 (couple);
(3) you are a U.S. citizen or a lawfully admitted alien living in the U.S.;
(4) you have cash resources under $1,500 (individual) or $2,250 (couple), *not including* the value of your house, car, personal effects, and household goods and furnishings;
(5) you do not have life insurance policies with a total value of more than $1,500 per person.

Because the first $20 of other monthly retirement income is not considered in computing these benefits, many persons receiving moderate retirement checks from other sources are eligible to receive Supplemental Security Income. For example, if you receive a Social Security check amounting to $120 a month, only $100 of that check will be counted in figuring out your Supplemental Security Income benefits. Therefore, you will receive an extra monthly check of $40, bringing your monthly cash income to a minimum $140. Since you already receive $120 from Social Security, the additional $40 will give you a total monthly income of $160.

If you are not receiving Supplemental Security Income and feel you may be eligible, apply at your local Social Security office. For the address and telephone number of the nearest office, follow the instructions on p. 133.

CIVIL SERVICE RETIREMENT

Most employees of the federal government are part of the civil service retirement system, and thus are eligible for civil service benefits when they retire. To qualify, you must complete five years of civilian service and must be part of the retirement system for at least one out of the two years prior to retirement. Any employee who has served at least fifteen years must retire at age seventy (that fifteen years includes creditable military service). Anyone who has not completed fifteen years of civilian service by age seventy may continue employment until he reaches that age unless separation is caused by a reduction in force or optional retirement or other similar changes in status.

An employee may choose optional retirement upon meeting a minimum combination of age and service: age sixty-two with five years of service; age sixty with twenty years of service; or age fifty-five with thirty years of service. An employee who becomes totally disabled after completing at least five years of civilian service is also eligible for retirement benefits.

Under the twenty-five-year discontinued-service retirement plan, any employee who is separated involuntarily (through no fault of the employee) may retire at an annuity slightly reduced for each full month the employee is under age fifty-five. The same holds true for twenty-year discontinued-service retirees who are separated after reaching age fifty and completing twenty years of service. In addition, any employee under age sixty-two who has completed five years of civilian service and is separated or transferred to a position in which that employee is not under the retirement system may elect deferred retirement, which begins on the employee's sixty-second birthday.

To apply for civil service retirement benefits, go to the personnel office of your employing agency and file an application for benefits. If you have been separated from civilian employment for more than thirty days, you should submit your application for retirement either directly to the Civil Service Commission, Washington, D.C. 20415 or to any regional or area Civil Service Commission office that may be listed in your telephone directory under U.S. Government.

INCOME TAX

The payment of income tax, while a civic duty, can also be a financial benefit. If you are sixty-five or older, the law grants you preferential treatment. It is thus very important that you fully understand and follow the proper method of filing your return.

The following questions and answers (adapted from Internal Revenue Service Publication 554, *Tax Benefits for Older Americans*) should prove helpful to you.

Q. Do I have to file an income tax return?

A. If you are sixty-five or older, you don't have to file an income tax return if you earned $2,800 or less. If you're married and either you or your spouse is sixty-five or older, you don't need to file a return if your combined income is $3,500 or less. If both you and your spouse are sixty-five or older and your combined income is $4,300 or less, you do not need to file a return.

However, if you are married and filing a separate return from your spouse, or a joint return if you live apart from your spouse, or if your husband or wife is claimed as a dependent by another taxpayer, you must file a return if you had a gross income of $750 or more.

If your gross income was low enough so that you are not required to file a return, but income tax was withheld from your pay, you should file a return *so that you will receive a refund* of the tax that was withheld. Do this even if you are claimed as a dependent by another taxpayer.

If neither you nor your spouse is required to file a return, but you file a joint return anyway to claim a refund of tax withheld, you may still be claimed as an exemption on the tax return of the person who lists you as a dependent.

Q. What is gross income?

A. Your gross income includes all the income you received in the form of money, property, and services that are not expressly exempt from tax by law.

If you're employed, your gross income is your *total* salary. If you are a landlord, it includes the total rent you receive *before* any rental expenses are deducted. For example, if you are single, sixty-five, and your only income is rents, and during the tax year you received gross rents of $3,600, but after deducting repairs, utilities, and depreciation your net rental income was only $1,400, you must still file a return because your gross income was more than $2,800. If you are self-employed, your gross income includes the total gross profit from your trade or business.

Self-employed persons must file a return when their net income is $400 or more or if they have uncollected Social Security tax on tips. Ask the IRS to send you Publication 533, *Information on Self-Employment Tax*, and Publication 531, *Reporting Your Tips for Federal Purposes*.

Q. If my spouse died during the year, do I need to file a return for him or her?

A. If you are the survivor, executor, or administrator of the estate of a person who died during the year, you may be required to file a return for that person. Ask for Publication 559, *Federal Tax Guide for Survivors, Executors and Administrators*.

Q. What is the exemption for age?

A. If you are sixty-five or older on the last day of the tax year, you're allowed an exemption of $750 in addition to the personal exemption of $750 to which every taxpayer is entitled. If your husband or wife is sixty-five or older on the last day of the tax year, you may claim both a regular exemption for him or her and an age exemption of $750 if you file a joint return. If your spouse had any gross income, you may claim his or her exemption only if you file a joint return. If your husband or wife died during the year, had no gross income, and wasn't a dependent of another taxpayer, you may claim his or her exemptions on a separate or joint return; however, if he or she had gross income and you claim his or her exemptions, you must file a joint return. If you remarried during the year, you may not claim exemptions for your deceased husband or wife. If you were divorced or legally separated at the end of the year you may not claim your former wife's or husband's exemptions even if you contributed all of her or his support. If death occurs before the end of the year, the full amount of the exemptions is allowed.

Q. My sister, who lives with me, is over sixty-five and blind. Can I claim blindness and age exemptions for her?

A. No. You can only claim the standard $750 exemption for your sister, even if she is a dependent.

Q. What is retirement income credit and how do I know if I qualify for it?

A. Persons who meet the prior-earned-income test

and who have any retirement income may be entitled to a credit against their income tax of up to 15 percent if they have retired or are sixty-five or older.

To meet the prior-earned-income test, you must have had more than $600 of earned income in each of any ten calendar years before the current year. Earned income is the gross amount of wages, salaries, or professional fees, and other amounts you received as compensation for personal services rendered. In some cases, professional, trade and business people do not meet the prior-earned-income test because of their level of personal services and capital outlay. Widows and widowers can sometimes claim the earned income of the deceased spouse who meets the prior-earned-income test.

If you are under sixty-five, retirement income includes only taxable income from a pension or annuity received from a public retirement system, such as a federal civil service retirement pension. If you are sixty-five or older before the end of the tax year, your retirement income includes your taxable income from pensions, annuities, interest, dividends, and rents when they are not earned income.

Q. Who is not eligible for retirement income credit?
A. Nonresident aliens; people who received Social Security, railroad retirement benefits, or any other pension or annuity excludable from gross income of $1,524 or more during the year if computing the retirement income separately, or of $2,286 if a husband and wife who are both

sixty-five or older compute the credit jointly; those under sixty-two with earned incomes of $2,424 or more during the year; and those sixty-two or older but under seventy-two who earned $2,974 or more during the year.

If you are seventy-two or older (you are considered seventy-two on the day before your seventy-second birthday), you may claim the credit if you otherwise qualify, regardless of the amount of income you earned.

Q. Are life insurance proceeds paid to me taxable?

A. Usually not. However, if payments are made to you in installments, you may be required to pay taxes on part of the proceeds.

Q. What income is not taxable?

A. Social Security benefits; railroad retirement benefits; public assistance or welfare payments; most compensation for injury or illness; gifts, benefits, or inheritances that do not produce taxable income; and veterans benefits such as disability compensation, pension payments, and insurance proceeds and dividends.

Q. Where can I get forms for filing my income tax?

A. Most banks, the post office, and all Internal Revenue Service offices have income tax return forms.

If you have further questions about filing your federal income tax return, call the IRS's tollfree telephone number in your area—check your local telephone directory or ask your directory assistance operator for the number—and ask for help with your problem or for the address of the nearest IRS office.

If you can't visit an IRS office, find out if there is a Taxmobile in your area—and, if there is, be sure to obtain a schedule of its visits. If there is no Taxmobile, perhaps a VITA (Volunteer Income Tax Assistance) volunteer can visit you at home. Finally, failing all other means of assistance, contact your neighborhood legal services office for help in filling out your return.

One final piece of advice: File your income tax return early. If you are filing for a refund, the earlier you send it in, the sooner you will have your refund.

VETERANS' BENEFITS

Veterans of the U.S. Armed Forces are eligible to receive a wide range of financial benefits—many related to the vital areas of health and housing. For example:

1. Veterans who are disabled by injury or disease incurred in, or aggravated by, military service can receive monthly compensation payments (ranging, in most instances from $28 to $495). In cases of serious disability, additional funds are provided for dependents.
2. Elderly veterans (defined by the Veterans Administration as veterans who are sixty-five or older) are eligible to receive a pension. Single veterans who earn less than $2,600 annually are entitled to *at least* $28 per month, while veterans with dependents who earn less than $3,800 annually can obtain *at least* $39 per month.
3. Elderly veterans in need of hospital care are entitled to admission to a VA hospital.

4. The VA will guarantee a loan for the purchase of a home or mobile home.
5. Veterans are entitled to burial in national cemeteries.

These are but a small sampling of the benefits available to veterans—and, very often, to their dependents and survivors. I strongly urge you to read *Federal Benefits for Veterans and Dependents*, a pamphlet prepared by the Veterans Administration Information Service and distributed by VA offices across the country. For a copy, and for answers to questions or problems you might have, call your nearest office. If there is none in your local area, ask the directory assistance (information) operator for the tollfree number of the office you should call.

2.

IF YOU WANT TO CONTINUE WORKING

There are many opportunities open to the older man or woman who is not interested in retirement. Traditionally, of course, most people were forced to leave their jobs at age sixty-five. If they then looked for new jobs, they found that the usual methods of competing were not open to them. Employers were looking for younger people.

In recent years, however, a new, healthier attitude toward employing the elderly has manifested itself, and new types of jobs have come into being. Many Americans now realize that an older, more experienced worker can bring to a job skills, knowledge and dependability that are lacking in many younger folks.

On the next several pages, I

briefly discuss some of the *paying jobs* currently available. Note that I've provided addresses, so you can write for more detailed information about those opportunities that particularly interest you.

FOSTER GRANDPARENT PROGRAM
Thousands of low-income people *age sixty and over* give love and attention to children who need some kind of help (see Chapter 2). Foster Grandparents *work twenty hours a week*, usually four hours a day. They are given an orientation before they begin work with the child care team at the institution or agency to which they are assigned. Pay is at least the federal minimum wage and participants receive a transportation allowance. Write: ACTION, Washington, D.C. 20525.

GREEN THUMB, INC.
Green Thumb employees work an average of *three days a week* to beautify highways, build parks, carry out conservation programs and help provide such community services as emergency home assistance and consumer education. You must be *at least fifty-five years old* and have a low annual income. Pay is at least the federal minimum wage. Transportation is arranged for employees. Write: Green Thumb, Inc., 1012 14th Street, N.W., Washington, D.C. 20005.

SENIOR AIDES
Low-income urban workers *fifty-five and over* work for community service agencies in jobs ranging from child care and adult education to home health and homemaker services. Pay is at least the federal minimum wage. Write: National Council of Senior

Citizens, 1511 K Street, N.W., Washington, D.C. 20005.

SENIOR COMMUNITY SERVICE PROJECT
Urban and rural low-income workers *fifty-five and over* perform a variety of community services—including work in community action programs, Social Security offices, public housing, and food and nutrition programs. They receive at least the federal minimum wage. Write: National Council on the Aging, 1828 L Street, N.W., Washington, D.C. 20036.

NRTA—AARP SENIOR COMMUNITY AIDES
The National Retired Teachers Association/ American Association for Retired Persons recruits, trains and finds part-time work for low-income people *fifty-five and over* in public service programs. Write: NRTA/AARP, 1909 K Street, N.W., Washington, D.C. 20006.

BUREAU OF THE CENSUS INTERVIEWERS
The Census Bureau will hire older people who are able to drive and read maps as part-time interviewers. Write: Bureau of the Census, U.S. Department of Commerce, Washington, D.C. 20233.

VOLUNTEERS IN SERVICE TO AMERICA (VISTA)
Americans of all ages work in impoverished urban and rural communities throughout the country, on Indian reservations, and in institutions for the mentally and physically handicapped. *Full-time volunteers work for a minimum of one year,* living in the community they serve; part-time workers reside at home, com-

muting to their projects. Volunteers receive a living allowance, medical care, travel expenses, and a sum that is set aside for payment when they complete service. Write: ACTION,Washington, D.C. 20525.

PEACE CORPS
The Peace Corps actively recruits older volunteers to serve overseas in education, agriculture, health, housing, public works, and community development programs. *Volunteers serve a minimum of two years*, receiving a living allowance, medical care, travel expenses, paid vacation, and an amount set aside for readjustment after service is completed. Write: ACTION, Washington, D.C. 20525.

Your community might offer *other paying opportunities that I haven't mentioned*, so look carefully in your own area. One worthwhile approach is to tell people you are looking for a job. Tell them if you're willing to accept reduced pay or part-time employment. Make the point that your skills, general experience and patience will enable you to perform types of work that you've never tried before.

In addition, there are numerous organizations that might be able to help you find a job. Consult your state employment service, the state committee on aging (see pp. 187–192 for addresses), labor unions, local senior centers, health and welfare councils, and employment agencies that cater especially to older workers (look in the yellow pages under employment agencies for senior citizens and for names like "Over 60 Employment Service").

Then, too, you might want to check the public

assistance department of social services in your locale. See if it hires healthy older people to provide personal foster care for older individuals who need daily assistance with dressing, cooking or other activities. Nearby hospitals and nursing homes might also provide full-time or part-time jobs.

Finally, consider contacting the nearest *Federal Job Information Center*. Located throughout the United States, FJICs provide announcements, application forms, and pamphlets about employment with the federal civil service. There are no civil service jobs specifically for the elderly; anyone may apply for any job opening in a federal government agency. (Compulsory retirement from the federal government comes at seventy.) But an FJIC official will be able to tell you what types of positions you are best suited for.

Check your telephone directory to see if there is an FJIC in your local area. If there isn't one nearby, ask your directory assistance (information) operator for the tollfree number you should call. Except in some parts of Alaska, California, Hawaii, Puerto Rico and Rhode Island, you may talk to an FJIC official over the phone at no expense.

People of all ages find volunteer work without remuneration to be a personally rewarding activity. Many elderly men and women accept *nonpaying jobs* that are similar to those I listed above. Here are some of the opportunities.

HOSPITAL VOLUNTEERS

Volunteers in Veterans Administration hospitals write letters, read, feed patients, and arrange recreational activities. Check with the nearest VA hospital or write Veterans Administration, Washington, D.C. 20420.

Other hospitals in your area usually have volunteer programs. Call and ask what you can do to assist the staff and patients.

SAVINGS BOND "SALESMEN"

The Department of the Treasury offers opportunities to volunteers to encourage the purchase of U.S. Savings Bonds. Write: Coordinator of Volunteer Activities, Savings Bond Division, U.S. Department of the Treasury, Washington, D.C. 20220.

COMMUNITY ACTION PROGRAMS

Both paid and volunteer workers help with community action programs in their area. For the address of the local community action agency, write: Office of Economic Opportunity, Washington, D.C. 20506.

EDUCATION

Retired teachers and teacher aides volunteer to help in public schools and in adult education programs. Find out about opportunities in your area through your local board of education.

Literacy councils in major cities train volunteers to teach reading to adults on a one-to-one basis. To find out if there is a literacy council in your area, write: National Affiliation for Literacy Advance, 1011 Harrison Street, Box 131, Syracuse, New York 13210.

SERVICE CORPS OF RETIRED EXECUTIVES (SCORE) AND ACTIVE CORPS OF EXECUTIVES (ACE)

Retired businessmen and women who have management expertise are recruited to provide counsel to the owners of small businesses and to community organizations that need management assistance. Write: ACTION, Washington, D.C. 20525.

RETIRED SENIOR VOLUNTEER PROGRAM (RSVP)

People *age sixty and over* volunteer to tutor children; assist in day care centers, courts, libraries and hospitals; counsel juvenile delinquents; and participate in many other community service activities. Shut-ins can sometimes serve as volunteers by providing telephone reassurance to others who cannot leave their homes, mending clothing for the needy, and helping in other ways. *Out-of-pocket expenses for transportation and meals frequently are compensated.* Write: ACTION, Washington, D.C. 20525

NATIONAL CENTER FOR VOLUNTARY ACTION (NCVA)

The NCVA functions as a clearinghouse for volunteer projects throughout the country. It collects and distributes information on successful projects, has information on organizations with technical expertise in various areas, and provides "how-to" advice on organizing volunteer service projects. Single copies of most publications are free. If you are interested in organizing a public service project, ask to be placed on the mailing list for *Voluntary Action News,* which announces the availability of new publications, and ask for material on your field of interest. Write: National Center for Voluntary Action, 1625 Massachusetts Avenue, N.W., Washington, D.C. 20336.

3.

HEALTH CARE

MEDICARE

Medicare is a program administered by the Social Security Administration, a division of the U.S. Department of Health, Education, and Welfare. It is a nationwide health insurance plan, available to almost every person sixty-five or older.*

Under Medicare, you are automatically entitled to *hospital insurance*, which helps pay for your care when you are hospitalized and for some health-related services, if you need them, after you leave the hospital. Although you will

---

*To be sure that you are eligible for Medicare, check with your local Social Security office. People who are not automatically eligible for Medicare are able to join the program by paying monthly premiums.

probably have to pay a small amount of the total cost of your hospital stay, you pay no monthly premium for Medicare hospital insurance. In effect, you already paid for this coverage through automatic payroll deductions during the years that you worked. The federal government feels that hospital insurance is a right of most people sixty-five and older.

In addition, you may choose to buy *medical insurance* at a small monthly premium charge. Under Medicare medical insurance, you pay an annual deductible fee and only 20 percent of your bills from doctors and from other medical services that you use. This is true whether you are treated in a doctor's office, in a hospital or at home.

Since there is variation both in the number of days you are covered under hospital and medical insurance and in the amount of coverage for each type of care, you should get a copy of *Your Medicare Handbook* from your local Social Security office or post office—if possible *before* you need Medicare benefits. Read through it, and if you still have questions, call the Social Security office. Each office has people who are trained to assist you with questions and problems about Medicare.

Here are some questions and answers that will help you understand the benefits you can receive from Medicare. Keep in mind that while hospital insurance is automatic in most cases, you can have coverage under medical insurance only if you choose to pay the monthly premium.

Q.   What if I can't pay bills that Medicare does not

pay for me through hospital and medical insurance?

A. Check with your local public assistance or welfare office. State programs, such as old age assistance or Medicaid, might defray some of your expenses. Your telephone operator can give you the number of public assistance or welfare office.

Q. Does medical insurance pay for personal care services—for example, a homemaker to assist me with daily needs such as eating, dressing, and getting around?

A. No. Medicare only pays for skilled health care provided by a hospital, skilled nursing facility, or a home health agency. If you are unsure whether the type of assistance you need is covered by Medicare, check with your Social Security office.

Q. How do I pay the small monthly medical insurance premium?

A. If you receive a monthly Social Security, railroad retirement, or civil service retirement check, the premium will be deducted automatically before you receive your check. If you do not receive any of these monthly retirement benefits, you must pay your premiums directly to the Social Security Administration.

Q. After I have received hospital or nursing care, do I have to file a claim for my benefits?

A. No. The hospital, nursing facility, or home health agency will make the claim and receive the Medicare payment directly. The Social Security Administration will notify you whenever a payment is made on your behalf.

Q. How long will Medicare hospital insurance pay

for extended nursing care in a skilled nursing facility?

A. Medicare will pay for this service *under certain conditions* for up to 100 days. During the first twenty days, all covered services are paid in full. Medicare will pay all but $9 of the charges for up to eighty more days of skilled nursing care. Check *Your Medicare Handbook* for a detailed description of extended care benefits.

Q. Can I choose my own doctor under the medical insurance program of Medicare?

A. You may go to any doctor you choose and receive medical help under Medicare. You and your doctor should decide whether medical insurance payments are to be made directly to your doctor or directly to you. If payment is made to you, then your doctor will bill you and you will pay your bill with the payment you receive from Medicare.

Q. Will Medicare's medical insurance pay for dental services, radiology and pathology services, and for an ambulance to take me to a hospital or nursing facility?

A. Medical insurance will pay only for dental services that involve surgery of the jaw or settings of the jaw and facial bones. It will not cover dental services such as filling or removing teeth or treatment of the gum areas or surgery related to these kinds of care. Radiology (such as x-rays) and pathology (such as blood and urine tests) services are completely paid by Medicare when you are a bed patient in a hospital. Medical insurance will pay 80 percent of all other services you receive as a hospital patient.

In most cases, medical insurance will help pay for ambulance service when it is needed. Restrictions on ambulance service are described in *Your Medicare Handbook*.

Q. Will medical insurance cover my treatment as an outpatient at a hospital?

A. Yes. Medicare will pay 80 percent of the reasonable charges for covered outpatient services after you have satisfied the deductible payment. Outpatient physical therapy and speech pathology services are also covered in most cases by the medical insurance.

Q. What services are not covered by hospital insurance?

A. No hospital insurance payments will be made for doctor bills, private duty nurses, convenience items (such as a telephone) while you are a hospital patient, cost of the first three pints of blood during a "benefit period" (for an explanation of "benefit period," consult *Your Medicare Handbook*), or homemaker services. However, if you have enrolled in the medical insurance program, you will receive help in paying your doctor bills.

Q. What services are not covered by medical insurance?

A. Medical insurance does not cover certain supplies and services such as routine checkups, prescription drugs, glasses and eye examinations to fit glasses, hearing aids, dentures and routine dental care, and orthopedic shoes. However, in some states, persons eligible for Medicaid will be provided with some of these supplies and services at no cost to them.

For further detailed information on Medicare's hospital and medical insurance plans, consult *Your Medicare Handbook.* Social Security offices can also provide you with claim forms used in filing for benefits. *Your Medicare Handbook* has full instructions for filling out whatever forms are required.

Note: *You should apply for a Medicare card and investigate your benefits under Medicare three months before you turn sixty-five. It generally takes several weeks to process your application. To apply, go to your local Social Security office with your birth certificate or other proof or age. Your proof-of-age document will be returned to you. If you can't go to a Social Security office, call the office listed in your telephone directory and arrange to apply for a Medicare card by mail. If there is no Social Security office in your area, call the office in the nearest large town collect. Employees have been authorized to accept collect calls from areas that do not have Social Security offices.*

MEDICAID

Medicaid is a medical assistance program that helps pay medical bills for low-income people. Although under the jurisdiction of the Social and Rehabilitation Service of the U.S. Department of Health, Education, and Welfare, each state administers the program for its citizens through county and city welfare, public assistance, or public health offices.

Eligibility requirements for Medicaid assistance vary from state to state. In general, however, you can assume that you are eligible for Medicaid if you receive, or are eligible to receive, public assistance (welfare) payments from your state. Since in some states certain other people also have the right to help from Medicaid (such as those whose incomes and resources are large enough to cover daily living expenses but not large enough to pay for medical care) you should contact your county or city public assistance, welfare, or public health office directly to determine if you are eligible. Check your local telephone directory for a listing *under your county or city government offices.* If you have difficulty locating the public assistance office, your directory assistance operator can tell you the correct telephone number to call. If you do not have a telephone, ask at your local post office for the address of the public assistance office and visit or write a letter inquiring about your eligibility for Medicaid.

All state Medicaid programs pay for at least the following services to people age sixty-five or older: inpatient hospital care; outpatient hospital services; other laboratory and x-ray services; skilled nursing home services; physicians' services wherever furnished; and home health care services. In addition, some states pay for dental care, prescribed drugs, eye glasses, clinic services, private duty nursing, physical therapy, podiatrists' and chiropractors' services, and care in mental institutions.

If you are part of Medicare's insurance program, Medicaid can also pay the costs of services not covered by Medicare.

The following questions and answers will give you a better understanding of the Medicaid program:

Q. Do I have to live in my state a certain length of time to qualify for Medicaid?
A. No. Medicaid is available without regard to length of residence in that state.
Q. May I choose my own doctor?
A. You may choose any doctor you wish as long as that doctor is willing to accept you as a patient.
Q. May I go to the hospital or nursing home of my choice?
A. You may go to any hospital or nursing home that meets federal standards. Except for a few smaller hospitals, almost every hospital in the U.S. has been federally certified. To determine whether a particular nursing home qualifies under Medicaid, contact the county or city public assistance, welfare, or public health office in the area where the nursing home is located.
Q. When I receive assistance that is covered by Medicaid, will the state pay my doctor, hospital, nursing home, or other service-provider directly, or will it pay me?
A. In most cases, payment will be made directly to the supplier of the service. For example, your doctor will report to the state welfare office that services have been provided to you under the Medicaid program. The state will then send the payment to your doctor. In some cases, however, the state will pay you and it will be your responsibility to pay the doctor.

Q. Do I have to pay for any part of the services provided to me under Medicaid?

A. In some cases, yes. However, before requiring you to pay any part of the costs of medical service, the state will take your income into consideration. If the state feels that your resources are below a certain level, you may not be required to shoulder any part of the cost of medical services under Medicaid.

Q. I have a health insurance policy with a private insurance company. Am I still eligible for Medicaid?

A. Yes, if you meet all eligibility requirements under the Medicaid program. However, your benefits under your private policy must be used before payment can be made under Medicaid. For example, if your private policy covers 80 percent of the cost of a particular service, Medicaid will pay only the remaining 20 percent of the cost of that service.

Q. Does Medicaid cover medical care administered to people aged sixty-five and older who are in institutions for mental diseases or tuberculosis?

A. Some states will pay for such care; others will not. Check with your local public assistance office to find out if your state will pay for medical care in such institutions.

For additional information, consult *Medicare . . . Medicaid: Which Is Which?*, a pamphlet available from the Superintendent of Documents, U.S. Government Printing Office, Washington, D.C. 20402. The cost is 40¢.

HEALTH MAINTENANCE ORGANIZATIONS

Health Maintenance Organizations, or HMOs, are designed to provide comprehensive health care to members. HMOs have a particular interest in preventive medicine, which is very important to older men and women. Individuals or groups (such as employees) pay a small monthly premium, which entitles them to complete hospital and medical care, usually at little or no cost to them. While HMOs generally prefer to have people enroll early in life so that their health care can be handled continuously by one group of health practitioners, some HMOs do accept new enrollees who are sixty-five or older. In addition, some HMOs exclude treatment for pre-existing chronic conditions such as diabetes and heart disease, while some do not. Check with the HMO in your area to determine whether you are eligible to join.

The relationship of Medicare and Medicaid to the local HMO should be ascertained by the prospective older enrollee. In some areas, the small HMO premium will cover those costs that Medicare's hospital insurance will not pay plus all of the services offered by Medicare's medical insurance plan. In other words, in some areas it *might* be less costly for a Medicare recipient to join an HMO rather than pay the monthly premiums for Medicare's medical insurance plan.

Each individual should check with the local HMO for eligibility requirements and a detailed description of coverage. Compare your local HMO plan with Medicare or Medicaid coverage so that the best possible coverage at the lowest possible cost can be selected.

If you don't know whether there is an HMO in

your area, write to the Group Health Association of America, 1717 Massachusetts Avenue, N.W., Washington, D.C. 20036 and ask for the address of the HMO nearest you.

PRIVATE INSURANCE PLANS
Some people elect to participate in health insurance plans offered by private insurance companies, even though they receive coverage under the Medicare program. While coverage differs depending on the insurance company chosen, in many cases private insurance plans will cover costs not paid by Medicare, such as the initial deductible and certain uncovered services. If you are eligible to receive Medicare benefits and you are interested in joining a private insurance plan, compare the coverage offered by the insurance company with Medicare benefits to be sure that the private insurance coverage is worth the monthly premiums you will pay. *Before signing a contract with a private insurance company, be sure that you read the contract thoroughly and that you understand the terms of the policy.*

COMMUNITY HEALTH CARE SERVICES
How can an individual learn about the full range of health and health-related services available in a community? Unfortunately, not every community has a central information and referral service.

However, there are several public agencies that might be able to tell you where you can get mental health, homemaker, visiting nurse, or other services. Ask about such services at your local welfare planning council such as the United Fund or United Way, if your area has an office. If not, try the local welfare or public health department. Sometimes the local Social Security office will be able to refer you to the appropriate service agency. Check your telephone directory for the telephone numbers of these offices. If you cannot find the numbers, ask your directory assistance operator for help.

How to Choose a Nursing Home

The first question to ask before choosing a nursing home either for yourself or a relative is: "Are there alternatives to nursing home care?" In the 1970s, the answer is "yes." In recent years, many communities have begun to provide services that can postpone—or even eliminate—the need for nursing home care. Among them are home health aides, therapists, visiting nurses, homemakers, and "meals on wheels." According to the Department of Health, Education, and Welfare, "The longer a person can cope with life outside an institution, the longer he or she usually retains dignity and a sense of independence." For this reason alone, health care should be provided at home if at all possible.

There are many elderly men and women, though, who do need nursing home care. Usually they are people who have difficulty dressing and feeding themselves and who live where neither their families nor communities can adequately look after them in their own homes. But what *kind* of nursing home? That depends on the special needs of each individual—and on his personal health coverage.

In general, there are two types of nursing home

facilities (as classified by Medicare and Medicaid programs):

1. An intermediate care facility is suited for the person who requires nursing assistance as well as help with such personal activities as dressing and eating. Medicare does not pay for intermediate care; in some states, Medicaid does.

2. A skilled nursing home offers round-the-clock nursing and medical supervision. Medicare pays for up to 100 days, but only if the resident has spent at least three days in a hospital and is referred to an extended care facility by a physician. Often, Medicaid will pay the costs incurred after 100 days.

Note: *A particular nursing home may qualify for both Medicaid and Medicare.*

Once you've selected the right type of home, the next problem is to choose the appropriate home itself. You can obtain the names of facilities in your area from many sources—the state branches of the American Nursing Home Association and the American Association of Homes for the Aging, the Social Security Office, your doctor and clergyman, the local health and welfare departments, etc. *But remember: different people and organizations will disagree about the quality of specific nursing homes.* You may want others to supply you with names, but *only you or those close to you can properly investigate and choose a home.*

Every place you consider should have a Nursing Home License, issued by the state—and every administrator should have a Nursing Home Administrator License (except in Arizona). *Don't consider un-licensed facilities.*

Next, call the homes on your list. Make sure each offers the kind of care you're interested in, and ask if expenses are covered by Medicare or Medicaid.

Now comes the tough part—visiting the nursing homes themselves. Think carefully before you go about what you want to see and what questions you want to ask. Here are some points to keep in mind:

- Plan to spend at least an hour at each home. You are deciding where you or someone close to you is going to live—and that's an important decision. *Make a thorough investigation!*
- Be sure to talk with the administrator. He or she sets the "tone" of the facility. Does he appear to be a trustworthy, humane person? Is he eager to show you his nursing home and answer your questions frankly—or does he appear to be hiding something? Inspect every floor. Don't be duped by an administrator who wants to show you only the best—you must see the whole facility to accurately judge its quality.
- Visit at midday and *talk with the residents.* If possible, join them for lunch. By noon, everyone should be awake and active, so you'll be able to assess the atmosphere in the home. (And you'll also have the opportunity to test the quality of the food.)

Now for some specific questions to ask yourself while you're touring each home:

1.   Is it conveniently located for visits by relatives, friends, and the resident's doctor?

2. Is it clean? Does it look attractive? Are there unpleasant odors?
3. Does the staff appear friendly and courteous? Do they seem *sincerely* interested in the well-being and happiness of the residents? Does the home have a cheerful atmosphere?
4. Is the home safe in case of fire? Are exit doors plainly marked and accessible, and can they be opened by an elderly person?
5. Was the building planned with the health and convenience of the residents in mind? Are there handrails in hallways, grab bars in bathrooms, and bells for summoning nurses by the beds?
6. In case of emergency, is a physician nearby? Are private physicians allowed to visit residents?
7. If you are considering a skilled nursing home, is a Registered Nurse responsible for the nursing staff?
8. Does the home have an arrangement with a local hospital for the transfer of residents in need of hospital care?
9. Are the residents alert and active? Can they wear their own clothes?

These questions, and many additional ones, are contained in a perceptive pamphlet, *Nursing Home Care.* For a copy, write to the Superintendent of Documents, U.S. Government Printing Office, Washington, D.C. 20402. The price is 40 cents.

Seven states have Nursing Home Ombudsman Demonstration Projects, established by the U.S. Department of Health, Education, and Welfare to investigate and mediate complaints filed against nursing homes. If you do not live in Idaho, Massachusetts, Michigan, Oregon, Pennsylvania, South Carolina or Wisconsin—where the projects are operating—and you have a complaint about a nursing home, contact your Social Security district office by telephone or letter. It will see that your complaint is investigated.

To find the telephone number of the Social Security District office, see p. 133. If you do not have a telephone, ask at your local post office for the address of the Social Security District office and write a letter explaining your problem. Or, direct complaints and inquiries to the Licensure and Certification Branch of your state health department in your state capital.

Each Social Security District office maintains a file detailing deficiencies in nursing homes and hospitals in the district, along with statements describing the intended improvements in deficient areas and timetables stating when improvements are to be expected. Contact your local Social Security office to find out the address of the District office. Then go to the District office and ask to see a copy of the deficiency reports for your area.

Below I've listed the addresses and telephone numbers of the existing Nursing Home Ombudsman Demonstration Project Offices:

Idaho
State Ombudsman for Nursing Homes
Idaho Office of Special Services
506 North Fifth
Boise, Idaho 83720
208-384-3833

Massachusetts
State Nursing Home Ombudsman
Executive Office of Elder Affairs
18 Tremont Street
Boston, Massachusetts 02108
617-727-7273

Michigan
Detroit
Detroit Local Unit
National Council of Senior
Citizens
Nursing Home Ombudsman
Demonstration Project
960 East Jefferson
Detroit, Michigan 48207
313-963-2526

Upper Peninsula
Upper Peninsula Nursing
Home Ombudsman Demon-
stration Project
107 10th Avenue
Menominee, Michigan 49858
906-864-2385

Elsewhere in Michigan
State Unit Director
National Council of Senior
Citizens
Nursing Home Ombudsman
Demonstration Project
2517 West Michigan Avenue
Lansing, Michigan 48917
517-482-7049

Oregon
Assistant State Ombudsman
for Nursing Homes
Suite 211
811 East Burnside
Portland, Oregon 97214
503-244-3528

Pennsylvania
Allegheny County
Allegheny County Unit
Pennsylvania Nursing Home
Ombudsman Demonstration
Project
Room 1403
State Office Building
300 Liberty Avenue
Pittsburgh, Pennsylvania 15222
412-565-2195

Elsewhere in Pennsylvania
Director
Pennsylvania Nursing Home
Ombudsman Demonstration
Project
Room 501
133 South 36th Street
Philadelphia, Pennsylvania
19104
215-238-7776

South Carolina
South Carolina Nursing Home
Ombudsman Demonstration
Project
915 South Main Street
Columbia, South Carolina
29201
803-758-2249

Wisconsin
Milwaukee County
Milwaukee Area Nursing
Home Ombudsman Demon-
stration Project

5th Floor
819 North 6th Street
Milwaukee, Wisconsin 53202
414-224-4386

Elsewhere in Wisconsin
Wisconsin Nursing Home

Ombudsman Demonstration
Project
Room 498
201 East Washington Avenue
Madison, Wisconsin 53702
608-266-8944

CHOOSING DOCTORS AND DENTISTS

For an elderly person, choosing a doctor or dentist is often a more arduous task than it is for younger people. We all want doctors with impeccable credentials, men and women of proven competence who have had expert training. But the aged, in addition, demand a doctor with a pleasant personality—someone who is obviously trustworthy, someone who can reassure them that he or she understands the loneliness that afflicts most older people from time to time. So, too, while geographical proximity to a doctor is a welcome convenience for the rest of us, it's a necessity for an elderly person who is dependent on public transportation.

Unfortunately, it can also be difficult to locate a doctor or dentist who likes to have older patients. Some physicians simply don't have the tolerance needed to treat people who might not move as quickly or talk as clearly as they once did.

How, then, do you go about selecting a physician?

A good place to begin is with friends and relatives. Ask them how they would rate their doctors, given the criteria I've mentioned. You might also write to the American Geriatrics Society, 10 Columbus

Circle, New York, New York 10019. Ask them for a list of doctors in your locale who are eager to accept older patients.

Keep financial considerations in mind. If you are eligible for Medicare, call the office of any doctor you are considering and, before making an appointment, ask if he will agree to "assignment payment" under Medicare. If he says yes, he will accept as full payment the amount that the Social Security Administration determines is reasonable payment for his services, and you will not be charged an additional fee. For example, if your doctor charges $20 for an office visit and the Social Security Administration determines that $15 is a reasonable payment for an office visit in your area, a doctor who will accept assignment payment will not charge you the remaining $5 fee. If the physician will not accept an assignment payment, check with other physicians in the area before choosing a doctor.

If you are eligible for Medicaid, ask your caseworker or your social worker at your local public assistance or welfare office for a list of doctors who will accept Medicaid patients. If you cannot get a referral, be sure to call the office of any doctor whom you are considering and ask if he accepts Medicaid patients. If the doctor you choose refuses to see Medicaid patients, and you decide to make an appointment anyway, you will have to pay the fees yourself.

Be sure to check with local public health agencies and welfare offices for the names of clinics and university dental schools in your area that might offer free or low-cost medical or dental services.

FOOD

The federal food stamp program is designed to aid individuals and families whose incomes fall below a specified level. If you are on public assistance or if your Social Security or other income is below a certain level, you may be entitled to exchange money for food coupons worth more than you pay. You may use these food stamps at most food stores to buy groceries (nonfood items such as soap and tobacco are excluded).

To apply for food stamps, go to your local public assistance or welfare office with documents showing where you live, how many people are in your family, how much income you and your family receive each month, and how much you and your family pay for doctors' bills and rent. If the office determines you are eligible for food stamps, it will figure out the number of stamps you may receive each month and the cost to you. If you are unable to travel to the public assistance office, ask someone else to go there for you. Simply provide a letter saying that he or she is authorized to apply for food stamps in your name.

Meals-on-Wheels, a community program located in many areas, brings food to some individuals who cannot leave their homes. Food stamps may be used to pay for these low-cost, nutritious meals; those who do not receive food stamps may be asked to pay a small fee for each meal. Call your local public agencies to find out if such a program exists in your area.

The National Nutrition Program for the Elderly provides at least one hot meal each day, five days a week, to persons sixty years old or over in group settings such as schools, senior citizens centers, and churches. While the emphasis is on feeding persons with low incomes, the program is also open to those who cannot shop or cook for themselves (whether because they have limited mobility or because they lack the skills to prepare adequate meals) and to those who neglect themselves and their diets because of feelings of loneliness. People are generally asked to pay what they can for the meals, but no one is excluded because of inability to pay. Each individual decides for himself whether or not to make a contribution. Check with your local public agencies or the state office on aging to find out if this program exists in your area.

If you cannot locate a food assistance program nearby, ask churches, synagogues, community service organizations, and youth groups whether they know of such programs. If none exist, they may want to start their own service projects.

For useful information on the purchasing and preparation of food, I recommend two pamphlets: *Food Guide for Older Folks* and *Family Food Budgeting*. The former costs 30¢, the latter 15¢. Both are available from the Superintendent of Documents, U.S. Government Printing Office, Washington D.C. 20402.

4.

PLANNING WHERE TO LIVE

WHAT ARE THE CHOICES?
As you approach your senior
years, it is vital to reassess your
housing needs. Will you be
comfortable and safe if you stay in
your present residence? Do you want
as much space as you needed when
the children were growing up? Can
you keep your home in optimum
condition? Do you have easy access
to public facilities, friends, and
essential services?

And, of course, you must
carefully consider finances. As a
retiree your income will probably
be considerably smaller than it was
during the working years. You must
make an honest appraisal of finances,
setting aside reasonable amounts
for emergencies. Realistically, any
decision about whether to move, or
where to move, must be based to a
large extent on financial considerations.

There is a wide variety of living arrangements to choose from. You can remain in your present home and leave it unchanged—or you can stay there and alter your quarters to make them more suitable for your future needs. You might want to live nearer to—or possibly with—relatives. Like many older people, you might prefer settling in a different environment—in a locale, for instance, that enjoys a warmer climate. Or you might decide to live in retirement housing that has been designed with the comfort and convenience of retired people in mind.

The decision to retain your home in its present condition is very attractive. It means that the problem of housing really is no problem at all. As a retiree, you will have the time to involve yourself more in the life of the community—church or synagogue activities, senior centers, civic organizations, volunteer projects, community action programs, etc.

But if you select one of the other housing options, you should acquaint yourself with problems and opportunities that might not have occurred to you.

First of all, if you decide to fix up your home or convert it into rental units, the federal government will grant you (as a senior citizen) a loan on special terms at low interest rates. You can learn about these loans at a bank or from the regional office of the U.S. Department of Housing and Urban Development (check the listing under U.S. Government in your telephone directory). Or, if you'd rather, write to the U.S. Department of Housing and Urban Development, Washington, D.C. 20410. The Farmers Home Administration of the U.S. Department of Agriculture makes home improvement loans to older homeowners in rural areas. Check your telephone directory for a county office in your area, or write to the Farmers Home Administration, U.S. Department of Agriculture, Washington, D.C. 20250.

If you are a homeowner and decide to change your permanent living arrangements, you will probably want either to lease or sell your house. Whichever option you select, think it out carefully in advance. *And make no commitment to rent or sell until you have selected another satisfactory living arrangement.* A competent appraiser can help you set a fair asking price for the sale of a home; a real estate agent can help you sell or lease it.

If you consider merging your household with that of your children, other relatives, or friends, be sure that every member of each household agrees to the plan and is willing to respect the rights to privacy of others and to share the tasks and responsibilities of the joint household. Many people find that, while they prefer to live near relatives, a joint living arrangement can be difficult for everyone. Careful thought and frank discussions before making such a move can help you avoid disastrous situations later.

A move to a new location should be as carefully considered as any other major change in lifestyle. While a city dweller might long for the quiet of a rural community, a permanent move away from the bustle and facilities of an urban area might bring boredom and inconvenience. On the other hand, a person from a small community might find that city living prevents the development of close associations that are so much a part of rural life. A temporary move to a new environment or climate, if it can be arranged, will show you how well a permanent move would suit you.

If you settle on retirement housing, your choices will range from clubs and cooperatives to homes for the aged. All retirement housing arrangements have one thing in common: In theory, they have been designed especially to accommodate the needs and wishes of older people. While their availability and their conformity to your particular needs will vary, most claim to provide older people with the desired features of comfort, convenience, and safety.

You should visit the various types of retirement housing before making a decision. In each case, check the site's location to see if it allows easy access to nearby community services and activities. Find out who operates the facility and whether concern for residents is a primary consideration. *Look at the accommodations in terms of your own needs. Ask what services you will get for the costs you are required to pay and read the contract carefully to be sure you agree with its conditions.* Walk around. Talk to people. Get the feel of the housing and the neighborhood. before you make a commitment.

WHAT KINDS OF RETIREMENT HOUSING ARE THERE?

In addition to convenience, comfort, and safety, some retirement housing plans provide essential health care and social services either on the premises or through special arrangements with the community. Some have group health insurance plans; most have intercom systems; many have lounges, social and recreational facilities and activities; and workshops;

and some arrange for residents to work with the local community on common interests and problems.

Retirement facilities should not look or feel like institutions. They might be limited to older people, or they might house younger people and families also. Before making a choice, remember that the housing you select might be your home for a long time. Choose a place that will make you feel at home.

Public or Low-cost Housing. People with low incomes should consider retirement housing sponsored by the community's housing authority or by a church. Each sponsor establishes its own admission requirements for low-cost housing. Besides an income ceiling, priority may be given to older people who are displaced by public improvements or who live in housing that falls below minimum standards. Check with your local housing authority or with a sponsoring church for admission requirements. Also inquire if there is a waiting list for new residents and, if there is, ask how long a person usually must wait for admission.

Apartments. Apartment houses built or converted for retirement living sometimes offer such amenities as housekeeping aid, optional community dining arrangements, and health programs. They provide the opportunity for privacy and independence within one's own apartment while relieving residents of many of the responsibilities of apartment living.

Most apartments for retired people are rented at a monthly rental charge. However, in cooperative apartments, each resident buys shares in a nonprofit corporation; in return, he or she is entitled to an apartment and a say about management. After buying shares in the corporation, the owner of a cooperative apartment simply pays a small monthly charge for maintenance of the building and grounds. A single mortgage covers the entire building or group of buildings.

In condominium housing, each resident carries a mortgage and shares in the ownership of common facilities. The condominium owner is much like any other homeowner, except that common facilities are owned by all residents.

Retirement Villages.   Homes in retirement villages or towns are usually restricted to people of at least a certain minimum age, although some stipulate only that at least one member of a family be above that age. Many retirement villages have a country club atmosphere, with golf courses, swimming pools, and lakes.

When you buy a home or cottage in a retirement village, you may find that complete maintenance of grounds and house for a fixed monthly fee is included in the contract. Some villages also offer social activities programs, health insurance plans, and health care facilities. If the village is located far from town, special transportation arrangements may be made for residents.

Mobile Homes.   Some people choose to retire to a trailer or mobile home, whether they want to travel or to install the trailer permanently in a mobile home park. Maintenance of a mobile home is easy, and some parks have community facilities that fulfill the needs of residents.

There are several disadvantages, however, to mobile home living. Depreciation of a mobile home is rapid and resale may be difficult. Some people don't like living as close to their neighbors as they often must in trailer parks. And services, beyond such things as hook-ups for water supplies, are rarely offered by mobile home parks.

Residence Clubs and Hotels.   Hotels and clubs that cater to older people generally offer furnished units, house-keeping services, community dining facilities, affiliation with local health services, and social and recreational activities. Residents who like the freedom of hotel living can find these arrangements convenient.

Some commercial hotels have been converted to serve retired people exclusively. Many of them are conveniently located near downtown shopping areas and community services. They frequently have common lounges and other rooms for social activities and usually have comfortable accommodations.

Some hotels, however, are unsafe and inconvenient for older people. They may be inexpensive, but you might find that rooms are restricted to double occupancy and that you are forced to live with a stranger. Maid service may be infrequent, safety precautions nonexistent, stairs steep, and elevators narrow.

As with other retirement housing, a temporary stay in a hotel or club can tell you whether you want to make it a permanent arrangement.

Homes for the Aged.   People who need help with the daily necessities of bathing, dressing, and walking, and who possibly require some nursing care, might prefer to move to homes for the aged. Here such services are provided both to comparatively well older people and to those who are ill and need skilled nursing care. (See pp. 164–170 for a discussion of nursing homes for those who need extensive nursing care.) The average age of applicants to homes for the aged is over seventy-five.

Multi-type Facilities. Some retirement areas are now developing facilities of several types—housekeeping, nonhousekeeping, nursing homes, and clubs—under the same roof. Thus, a temporary or permanent change in the needs of a resident can be handled easily within the same complex, necessitating a simple move from, say, a housekeeping unit to a nursing home when a resident becomes ill.

WHERE TO FIND OUT ABOUT RETIREMENT HOUSING

Before making a decision about retirement housing, go to your local library and ask to see a copy of *Guide to Retirement Living*, by Paul Holter (Rand McNally, 1973). It includes information on tax benefits, how to handle money, selling your home, and other important issues. *A Naional Directory of Housing for Older People*, prepared by the National Council of the Aging, contains an excellent guide to the selection of housing and checklists of what to look for when you are deciding whether to remain where you are or move elsewhere. These books may help you avoid problems on matters you may not even think of when you are selecting living arrangements.

You may not be able to get a list of all retirement housing in your locale from one agency. However, you should check with the following groups and agencies for the names, addresses, and descriptions of the housing that interests you. Then, before making a commitment, visit the areas and talk with residents. Remember: a decision should be made only after careful thought and a realistic appraisal of your finances.

Local housing authority (check your telephone directory under city government listings or ask your directory assistance operator for help; or write to your mayor or city hall for an address)—for public housing and moderate-income housing.

Public assistance or welfare office (for telephone number, proceed as above)—for public housing.

Churches and philanthropic groups such as B'nai B'rith, Kiwanis, and trade unions—for private, nonprofit housing.

Health and welfare councils or councils of social agencies of the United Fund or United Way (check your telephone directory under United Fund or United Way)—for all retirement housing.

In addition, ask at your local library for copies of *Best Places to Live When You Retire*, by Huesinkveld and Musson; *Retirement Facilities Register*, by the Active Retirement Executive Association; and *A National Directory on Housing for Older People*, by the National Council on the Aging. I especially recommend the latter volune. It features a state-by-state discussion of retirement housing, including the names and locations of facilities.

5.

WHERE TO GO FOR HELP

Sometimes you may feel you
have been treated unfairly. On
other occasions you may simply
not know where to turn for help
with a problem that does not seem to
fit into any of the usual categories.
Here are some of the people and
organizations you should consult
when such situations arise.

FEDERAL AND STATE OFFICES ON AGING

The Administration on Aging,
an office of the U.S. Department of
Health, Education, and Welfare, is
an excellent information and referral
agency. It publishes several
booklets that provide a clear picture
of many types of programs for older
Americans throughout the United
States. Your community may
already sponsor some of these

programs. If it does not, why not organize a project to assist other older Americans in your area? Interesting ideas for projects are discussed in such booklets as *Are You Planning on Living the Rest of Your Life?*, *Employment and Volunteer Opportunities for Older People*, *To Find the Way*, *Guidelines for a Telephone Reassurance Service*, and *Project Helping Wheels.* Most of the Administration's publications are free of charge. Write: Administration on Aging, U.S. Department of Health, Education, and Welfare, Washington D.C. 20201.

In addition, each state maintains an office on aging to serve you, and local offices are currently being opened. Your state office may have a list of local home help services that can assist you with the chores such as gardening and home repairs; transportation services to increase your mobility; health services to screen you for undetected illnesses; counseling services to help you find solutions to personal problems; telephone reassurance projects staffed by people who will call you on a regular basis; and other community programs to aid you in seeking employment, recreation, a balanced diet, and companionship.

Below are the addresses and telephone numbers of state offices. If you decide to call your state agency, check your local telephone directory to be sure that the telephone number is within your local calling area. If it is not, you may want to write a letter rather than make a long-distance call.

STATE OFFICE

Alabama
Commission on Aging
740 Madison Avenue
Montgomery 36104
(205) 269-8171

Alaska
Office on Aging
Department of Health and
Social Services
Pouch H
Juneau 99801
(907) 586-6153

Arizona
Bureau on Aging
Department of Economic
Security
2721 North Central, Suite 800
Phoenix 85004
(602) 271-4446

Arkansas
Office on Aging
Department of Social and
Rehabilitation Services
4313 West Markham
Hendrix Hall
P. O. Box 2179
Little Rock 72203
(501) 371-2441

California
Commission on Aging
Health and Welfare Agency
926 J Street, Suite 701
Sacramento 95814
(916) 322-5630

Colorado
Division of Services for
the Aging
Department of Social Services
1575 Sherman Street
Denver 80203
(303) 892-2651

Connecticut
Department on Aging
90 Washington Street
Room 318
Hartford 06115
(203) 566-2480

Delaware
Division of Aging
Department of Health and
Social Services
2413 Lancaster Avenue
Wilmington 19805
(302) 571-3480

District of Columbia
Division of Services to the Aged
Department of Human
Resources
1329 E Street, N.W.
Munsey Building, 10th Floor
Washington, D. C. 20004
(202) 638-2406

Florida
Division on Aging
Department of Health and
Rehabilitative Services
1317 Winewood Boulevard
Tallahassee 32301
(904) 488-4797

STATE OFFICE

Georgia
Office of Aging
Department of Human
Resources
1372 Peachtree Street, N.E.
Suite 301
Atlanta 30309
(404) 892-1243

Hawaii
Commission on Aging
1149 Bethel Street
Room 311
Honolulu 96813
(808) 548-2593

Idaho
Office on Aging
Department of Special Services
State House Mail
506 North 5th Street
Boise 83707
(208) 384-3833

Illinois
Department on Aging
2401 West Jefferson Street
Springfield 62706
(217) 525-5773

Indiana
Indiana Commission on Aging
and Aged
Graphic Arts Building
215 North Senate Avenue
Indianapolis 46202
(317) 633-5948

Iowa
Commission on the Aging
415 West 10th Street
Jewett Building
Des Moines 50319
(515) 281-5187

Kansas
Department of Social and
Rehabilitation Services
Division of Social Services
Services for the Aging Section
State Office Building
Topeka 66612
(913) 296-3465

Kentucky
Commission on Aging
403 Watping Street
Frankfort 40601
(502) 564-6930

Louisiana
Bureau of Aging Services
P.O. Box 44282, Capitol
Station
Baton Rouge 70804
(504) 389-6713

Maine
Bureau of Maine's Elderly
Community Services Unit
Department of Health and
Welfare
State House
Augusta 04330
(207) 289-2561

STATE OFFICE

Maryland
Commission on Aging
State Office Building
1123 North Eutaw Street
Baltimore 21201
(301) 383-2100

Massachusetts
Executive Office of Elder
Affairs
State Office Building
18 Tremont Street
Boston 02108
(617) 727-7273

Michigan
Office of Services to the
Aging
1026 E. Michigan Avenue
Lansing 48912
(517) 373-8320

Minnesota
Governor's Citizens Council
on Aging
690 N. Robert Street
St. Paul 55155
(612) 296-2770

Mississippi
Council on Aging
P.O. Box 5136
Fondren Station
Jackson 39216
(601) 354-6590

Missouri
Office of Aging
Department of Social Services
Broadway State Office Bldg.
P.O. Box 570
Jefferson City 65101
(314) 751-3074

Montana
Aging Services Bureau
Department of Social and
Rehabilitation Services
P.O. Box 1723
Helena 59601
(406) 449-3124

Nebraska
Commission on Aging
State House Station 94784
Lincoln 68509
(402) 471-2307

Nevada
Division of Aging
Department of Human
Resources
201 S. Fall Street
Carson City 89701
(702) 882-7855

New Hampshire
Council on Aging
P.O. Box 786
14 Depot Street
Concord 03301
(603) 271-2751

STATE OFFICE

New Jersey
Office on Aging
Department of Community
Affairs
P.O. Box 2768
363 West State Street
Trenton 08625
(609) 292-3765

New Mexico
Commission on Aging
408 Galisteo-Villagra Bldg.
Santa Fe 87501
(505) 827-5258

New York City Office
New York State Office for
the Aging
2 World Trade Center
Room 5036
New York 10047
(212) 488-6405

New York
New York State Office for
the Aging
New York State Executive
Dept.
855 Central Avenue
Albany 12206
(518) 457-7321

North Carolina
Governor's Coordinating
Council on Aging
Department of Human

Resources
Administration Building
213 Hillsborough Street
Raleigh 27603
(919) 829-3983

North Dakota
Aging Services
Social Services Board
State Capital
Bismarck 58501
(701) 224-2577

Ohio
Commission on Aging
34 North High Street
3rd Floor
Columbus 43215
(614) 466-5500

Oklahoma
Special Unit on Aging
Department of Institutions
Social and Rehabilitative
Services
Box 25352, Capitol Station
Oklahoma City 73125
(405) 521-2281

Oregon
Program on Aging
Human Resources Department
315 Public Service Building
Salem 97310
(503) 378-4728

STATE OFFICE

Pennsylvania
Bureau for the Aging
Office of Adult Programs
Department of Public Welfare
Capital Associates Building
7th and Forester Streets
Harrisburg 17120
(717) 787-5350

Puerto Rico
Gericulture Commission
Department of Social Services
Apartado 11697
Santurce 00910
(809) 725-8015

Rhode Island
Division of Services for Aging
Department of Community
Affairs
150 Washington Street
Providence 02903
Dial (401) 528-1000 and
ask for 277-2858

South Carolina
Commission on Aging
915 Main Street
Columbia 29201
(803) 758-2576

South Dakota
Program on Aging
Department of Social Services
Box 130, St. Charles Hotel
Pierre 57501
(605) 224-3656

Tennessee
Commission on Aging
306 Gay Street
S & P Building
Room 102
Nashville 37201
(615) 741-2056

Texas
Governor's Committee on Aging
P.O. Box 12786
Capitol Station
Austin 78711
(512) 475-2717

Utah
Division of Aging
Department of Social Services
345 South 6th Street
Salt Lake City 84102
(801) 328-6422

Vermont
Office on Aging
Department of Human Services
126 Main Street
Montpelier 05602
(802) 828-3471

Virginia
Office on Aging
Division of State Planning
and Community Affairs
9 North 12th Street
Richmond 23219
(804) 770-7894

STATE OFFICE

Virgin Islands
Commission on Aging
P.O. Box 539
Charlotte Amalie
St. Thomas 00801
(809) 774-5884

Washington
Office on Aging
Department of Social and
Health Services
P.O. Box 1788
410 West Fifth
Olympia 98504
(206) 753-2502

West Virginia
Commission on Aging
State Capitol

Charleston 25305
(304) 348-3317

Wisconsin
Division on Aging
Department of Health and
Social Services
1 West Wilson Street
Room 686
Madison 53702
(608) 266-2536

Wyoming
Adult Services
Department of Health and
Social Services
Division of Public Assistance
and Social Services
New State Office Building, West
Cheyenne 82002
(307) 777-7561

FEDERAL INFORMATION CENTERS

Federal Information Centers, which are part of the U.S. General Service Administration, can help you with *any* question or problem relating to the federal government. They are one-step information centers, designed to make it unnecessary for you to go from office to office in a federal agency before you stumble across the person qualified to assist you. At the FIC, a staff member will research your question. If he or she cannot provide you with the information you need, you'll be told who *will* be able to deal with your problem. Want to know how to apply for food stamps? Where to get a copy of your birth certificate? These are easy ones for the FIC.

Note that the Federal Information Centers employ bilingual personnel to assist those who do not speak English. They also stock a wide variety of booklets (available free of charge or for a low price) about consumer products and government programs.

There are presently thirty-six FICs located in major metropolitan areas. Residents of thirty-seven other areas can make tollfree telephone calls to Federal Information Centers by calling the appropriate tieline telephone number.

Dial This Local
Telephone Number
If You Live In . . .

Arizona
Phoenix
261-3313
Federal Building
230 N. First Ave.
85025

California
Los Angeles
688-3800
Federal Building
300 N. Los Angeles St.
90012

Sacramento
449-3344
Federal Building—
U.S. Courthouse
650 Capitol Hall
95814

San Diego
293-6030
202 C Street 92101

San Francisco
556-6600
Federal Building
U.S. Courthouse
450 Golden Gate Ave.
94102

Colorado
Denver
837-3602
Federal Building
U.S. Courthouse
1961 Stout Street
80202

Florida
Miami
350-4155
Federal Building
51 Southwest First Ave.
33130

St. Petersburg
893-3495

William C. Cramer
Federal Building
144 First Ave., S. 33701

Georgia
Atlanta
526-6891
Federal Building
275 Peachtree St., N.E. 30303

Hawaii
Honolulu
546-8620
U.S. Post Office
Courthouse &
Customhouse
335 Merchant St. 96813

Illinois
Chicago
353-4242
Everett McKinley
Dirksen Building
219 South Dearborn St.
60604

Indiana
Indianapolis
633-8484
Federal Building
U.S. Courthouse
46 E. Ohio St. 46204

Kentucky
Louisville
582-6261
Federal Building
600 Federal Place 40202

Louisiana
New Orleans
527-6696
Federal Building
Room 1210
701 Loyola Ave. 70113

Maryland
Baltimore
962-4980
Federal Building
31 Hoplins Plaza 21201

Massachusetts
Boston
223-7121
John Fitzgerald Kennedy
Federal Building
Government Center 02203

Michigan
Detroit
226-7016
Federal Building
U.S. Courthouse
231 West Lafayette St. 48226

Minnesota
Minneapolis
625-2073
Federal Building
U.S. Courthouse
230 South Fourth St. 55401

Missouri
Kansas City
374-2466
Federal Building

601 East Twelfth St.
64106

St. Louis
622-4106
Federal Building
1520 Market St. 63103

Nebraska
Omaha
221-3353
Federal Building
U. S. Post Office
& Courthouse
215 North 17th St.
68102

New Jersey
Newark
645-3600
Federal Building
970 Broad St. 97102

New Mexico
Albuquerque
766-3091
Federal Building
U. S. Courthouse
500 Gold Avenue, S.W.
87101

New York
Buffalo
842-5770
Federal Building
111 West Huron St. 14202

New York
264-4464

Federal Office Building
U.S. Customs Court
26 Federal Plaza 10007

Ohio
Cincinnati
684-2801
Federal Building
550 Main St. 45202

Cleveland
522-4040
Federal Building
1240 East Ninth St.
44199

Oklahoma
Oklahoma City
231-4868
U.S. Post Office &
Federal Office Building
201 N.W. 3rd St.
73102

Oregon
Portland
221-2222
208 U.S. Courthouse
620 Southwest Main St.
97205

Pennsylvania
Philadelphia
597-7042
William Green Jr.
Federal Building
600 Arch St.
19106

Pittsburgh
644-3456
Federal Building
1000 Liberty Ave. 15222

Tennessee
Memphis
534-3285
Clifford Davis
Federal Building
167 N. Main St. 38103

Texas
Fort Worth
334-3624
Fritz Garland Lanham
Federal Building
819 Taylor St.
76102

Houston
226-5711
Federal Building
U. S. Courthouse
515 Rusk Ave. 77002

Utah
Salt Lake City
524-5353
Federal Building
U.S. Post Office,
Courthouse
125 So. State St. 84138

Washington
Seattle
442-0570
Arcade Plaza
1321 Second Ave. 98101

FIC TOLLFREE TIELINE NUMBERS

If You Are In . . .	*Dial Tollfree . . .*
Alabama	
Birmingham	322-8591
Mobile	438-1421
Arkansas	378-6177
Little Rock	
Arizona	662-1511
Tucson	
California	
San Jose	275-7422
Colorado	
Colorado Springs	471-9491
Pueblo	544-9523

Connecticut	527-2617
Hartford	624-4720
New Haven	
Florida	522-8531
Fort Lauderdale	354-4756
Jacksonville	229-7911
Tampa	833-7566
West Palm Beach	
Iowa	
Des Moines	282-9091
Kansas	232-7229
Topeka	263-6931
Wichita	
Missouri	233-8206
St. Joseph	
New Jersey	
Trenton	396-4400
New Mexico	
Santa Fe	983-4743
New York	
Albany	463-4421
Rochester	546-5075
Syracuse	476-8545
North Carolina	
Charlotte	376-3600
Ohio	
Akron	375-5475
Columbus	221-1014
Dayton	223-7377
Toledo	244-8625

Oklahoma
Tulsa   584-4193

Pennsylvania
Scranton   346-7081

Rhode Island
Providence   331-5565

Tennessee
Chattanooga   265-8231

Texas
Austin   472-5495
Dallas   749-2131
San Antonio   224-4471

Utah
Ogden   399-1347

Washington
Tacoma   383-5230

Wisconsin
Milwaukee   271-2273

LEGAL ASSISTANCE

If you have a problem that requires the services of a lawyer, you might want to contact your local bar association. Its staff can tell you if you qualify for free legal assistance, or, if your income is too large to entitle you to free aid, the staff will be able to refer you to a lawyer in private practice. Your local bar association should be listed in your telephone directory under the name of your city or county. If none exists in your area, contact the state bar association, listed below.

The U.S. Office of Economic Opportunity has established legal services offices in 900 communities across America to provide legal assistance to people who cannot afford to retain private lawyers. If your retirement income is small enough to entitle you to such services, and if there is no legal services office near you, write to the National Senior Citizens Law Center, 1709 West 8th Street, Los Angeles, California.

STATE BAR ASSOCIATION

Alabama State Bar
P.O. Box 2106
Montgomery 36103
(205) 269-1515

Alaska Bar Assn.
P.O. Box 279
Anchorage 99510
(907) 272-7469

State Bar of Arizona
858 Security Bldg.
Phoenix 85004
(602) 252-4804

Arkansas Bar Assn.
408 Donaghey Bldg.
Little Rock 72201
(501) 375-4605

State Bar of California
601 McAllister St.
San Francisco 94102
(415) 922-1440

Colorado Bar Assn.
200 W. 14th Ave.
Denver 80204
(303) 222-9421

Connecticut Bar Assn.
15 Lewis St.
Hartford 06103
(203) 249-9141

Delaware State Bar Assn.
Ste. 701 Market Tower
Wilmington 19801
(302) 656-3371

Bar Assn. of the District of
Columbia
1819 H St., N.W.
Washington, D.C. 20006
(202) 223-1480

The Florida Bar
Tallahassee 32304
(904) 222-5286

STATE BAR ASSOCIATION

State Bar of Georgia
813 American Federal Bldg.
Macon 31201
(912) 745-6579

Bar Assn. of Hawaii
P.O. Box 26
Honolulu 96810
(808) 537-1868

Idaho State Bar
P.O. Box 835
Boise 83701
(208) 342-8958

Illinois State Bar Assn.
Illinois Bar Center
Springfield 62701
(217) 525-1760

Indiana State Bar Assn.
330 Bankers Trust Bldg.
Indianapolis 46204
(317) 639-5465

Iowa State Bar Assn.
404 Equitable Bldg.
Des Moines 50309
(515) 243-3179

Kansas Bar Assn.
P.O. Box 1037
Topeka 66601
(913) 234-5696

Kentucky State Bar Assn.
243 State Capitol
Frankfort 40601
(502) 564-3795

Louisiana State Bar Assn.
101 Supreme Court Bldg.
New Orleans 70112
(504) 522-9172

Maine State Bar Assn.
P.O. Box 788
Augusta 04330
(207) 622-7523

Maryland State Bar Assn.
905 Keyser Bldg.
Baltimore 21202
(301) 685-7878

Massachusetts Bar Assn.
One Center Plaza
Boston 02108
(617) 523-4529

State Bar of Michigan
306 Townsend St.
Lansing 48933
(517) 372-9030

Minnesota State Bar Assn.
100 Minnesota Federal Bldg.
Minneapolis 55402
(612) 335-1183

Mississippi State Bar
P.O. Box 1032
Jackson 39205
(601) 948-4471

The Missouri Bar
326 Monroe St.
Jefferson City 65101
(314) 635-4128

STATE BAR ASSOCIATION

Montana Bar Assn.
P.O. Box 906
Helena 59601
(406) 442-7660

Nebraska State Bar Assn.
1019 Sharp Bldg.
Lincoln 68508
(402) 477-7717

State Bar of Nevada
P.O. Box 1291
Reno 89504
(702) 329-0252

New Hampshire Bar Assn.
77 Market St.
Manchester 03101
(603) 669-4869

New Jersey State Bar Assn.
172 W. State St.
Trenton 08608
(609) 394-1101

State Bar of New Mexico
26 Supreme Court Bldg.
Santa Fe 87501
(505) 827-2411

New York State Bar Assn.
One Elk St.
Albany 12207
(518) 449-5141

The North Carolina State Bar
Justice Bldg.
Raleigh 27611
(919) 832-0518

North Carolina Bar Assn.
1025 Wade Ave.
Raleigh 27605
(919) 828-0561

State Bar Assn. of North
Dakota
314 MDU Office Bldg.
Bismarck 58501
(701) 255-1404

Ohio State Bar Assn.
33 W. 11th Ave.
Columbus 43201
(614) 421-2121

Oklahoma Bar Assn.
P.O. Box 53036
Oklahoma City 73105
(405) 524-2365

Oregon State Bar
808 S.W. 15th Ave.
Portland 97205
(503) 229-5476

Pennsylvania Bar Assn.
P.O. Box 186
Harrisburg 17108
(717) 238-6715

The Bar Assn. of Puerto Rico
P.O. Box 1900
San Juan 00903
(809) 724-3358

Rhode Island Bar Assn.
17 Exchange St.
Providence 02903
(401) 421-5740

STATE BAR ASSOCIATION

South Carolina State Bar
P.O. Box 11297
Capitol Station
Columbia 29211
(803) 256-8067

South Carolina Bar Assn.
1515 Green St.
Columbia 29208
(803) 777-4155

State Bar of South Dakota
222 E. Capitol Ave.
Pierre 57501
(605) 224-7554

Tennessee Bar Assn.
Ste. 600
1717 W. End Bldg.
Nashville 37203
(615) 329-1601

State Bar of Texas
P.O. Box 156
Woodville 75979
(713) 283-3711

Utah State Bar
203 Kearns Bldg.
Salt Lake City 84101
(801) 322-5273

Vermont Bar Assn.
P.O. Box 25

Charlotte 05445
(802) 425-2861

The Virginia Bar Assn.
School of Law
Univ. of Virginia
Charlottesville 22901
(703) 924-3416

Virginia State Bar
5th & Franklin Sts.
Richmond 23219
(703) 770-2061

Washington State Bar Assn.
505 Madison
Seattle 98104
(206) 622-6054

The West Virginia State Bar
E-404, State Capitol
Charleston 25322
(304) 346-8414

State Bar of Wisconsin
402 W. Wilson St.
Madison 53703
(608) 257-3838

Wyoming State Bar
275 N. Bent
Powell 82435
(307) 754-2934

One last suggestion about legal assistance. The pamphlet *"You, the Law and Retirement"* will tell you why, how and when you should see a lawyer. For a copy, write to the Administration of Aging, U.S. Department of Health, Education and Welfare, Washington, D.C. 20201.

AGE DISCRIMINATION IN EMPLOYMENT
Some older workers who are not yet sixty-five find that they are discriminated against simply because of age. Those who are employed are sometimes denied promotions, or they may be discharged from their jobs. And older job applicants often can find no one who will hire them.

Such discrimination on the basis of age is illegal. If you are under sixty-five and feel that you are being treated unfairly because of your age, notify your local Wage and Hour office. Addresses are listed in most telephone directories under "U.S. Government, Department of Labor, Wage and Hour Division." If you are unable to find a listing in your telephone directory, write to the U.S. Department of Labor, Wage and Hour Division, Washington, D.C. 20210. Your inquiry will be kept confidential.

HOUSING INSPECTION
If you are a tenant in a house or apartment owned by someone else and you feel that the owner has refused to take care of the building properly (for example, the toilet does not flush or plaster is falling from the ceiling), call your city or county housing inspector and ask to have your home inspected. Check your telephone directory under your city or county listings for the number of the housing inspector's

office. If you cannot locate the number, call your city or town hall and ask the operator for the number.

NEWSPAPERS

Sometimes the only way to obtain help is to publicize your problem. Many newspapers feature an "action line" column, which tries to help solve the problems of individual readers. If your newspaper does not have such a column, call and say that you want to speak to a reporter who is interested in the concerns of older people. You might be surprised by the results. In one major city, for example, many elderly, handicapped people were unable to buy food stamps because of a new requirement that all food stamp identification cards include a photograph of the recipient. The mobile photography unit that was to come to their homes was weeks behind schedule and they were unable to go to the local welfare office to have their pictures taken. A few days after an article appeared in a local newspaper, every one of those people had the new identification card.

If you feel that your problem is one that might be solved with the help of publicity, call your local newspaper, television, or radio station and ask to speak to someone who might be willing to publicize your concern.

PRIVATE ORGANIZATIONS

Ralph Nader's Retired Professional Action Group is particularly interested in problems that older Americans encounter as consumers. Land sales, rents, housing for the elderly, hearing aids, nursing homes, health care, and similar topics have been investigated by the group. Letters about problems unrelated to issues under investigation are forwarded by the group to the appropriate office. Write to the Retired Professional Action Group, 2000 P Street, N.W., Washington, D.C. 20036.

The Gray Panthers, an action organization advocating social and political changes for the elderly, is affiliated with the Retired Professional Action Group. The Panthers want to know your views on matters of interest to the aged, and they seek your time and energy to help solve problems. Your concern may be with age discrimination in employment, the difficulties older people experience in obtaining adequate transportation services, the refusal of some banks to offer banking services to older people, or any other problem encountered by people because of their age. The Gray Panthers demonstrate, lobby, and organize on the local level to bring about changes.

Write to the national office—Gray Panthers, 3700 Chestnut Street, Philadelphia, Pennsylvania 19104— to find out if there is a Gray Panther office in your area. Ask to have your name added to the mailing list of the national Gray Panther newsletter, *Network.* It will help you keep in touch with Panther activities throughout the nation. Membership in the organization is free, although contributions are always welcome.

COMMUNITY SERVICES

Many communities have local services such as hot lunch programs, telephone reassurance projects, special transportation, and organizations that join younger and older citizens in mutual activities. Check with local chapters of the United Fund/United Way, churches, synagogues, universities, and youth or- ganizations such as the Girl Scouts and Boy Scouts to find out what services are available to you in your community. Senior Citizen Centers, offering a wide variety of services to older people, exist in many communities across the country. To find out if one is located near your home, call your local office on aging or department of social services or the state agency on aging.

CALL FOR ACTION

Call for Action is an important program that meets the needs of confused and distraught citizens in many cities across the country. Sponsored mostly by local radio or television stations, it is staffed by volunteers who will identify the proper public or private agency to answer your questions, tell you where you might get free services and assist you in many other ways. Volunteers will even help you fight city hall if the need arises. In cases where neither you nor the Call for Action volunteers can get satisfactory assistance from a public or private agency, sponsoring radio or television stations might broadcast editorials and interviews documenting the agency's failure to perform.

Unfortunately, Call for Action cannot support a tollfree telephone service. Therefore, if you intend to contact Call for Action outside your local area, be prepared to place a long-distance call. Below, I have listed the locations and telephone numbers of par- ticipating chapters.

If You Are In	Dial This Local Number	Sponsoring Station
Alabama		
Birmingham	(205)323-1668	WYDE
Arizona		
Tucson	(602)623-3471	KTKT
Arkansas		
Little Rock	(501)375-4449	KARK-TV
California		
Sacramento	(916)766-7741	KCRA-TV
San Diego	(714)263-4469	KGTV
San Francisco	(415)398-5225	KABL
Colorado		
Denver	(303)623-2285	KLZ
Connecticut		
New Haven	(203)281-1733	WELI
District of Columbia		
D.C. Metropolitan Area	(202)393-3333	——
Florida		
Orlando	(305)241-1491	WDBO
Illinois		
Chicago	(312)644-0560	WIND
Peoria	(309)673-1919	WRAU-TV
Indiana		
Fort Wayne	(219)742-7277	WOWO
Indianapolis	(317)639-4648	WFBM
Maryland		
Baltimore	(301)366-5900	WBAL

IF YOU ARE IN	DIAL THIS LOCAL NUMBER	SPONSORING STATION
Massachusetts		
Boston	(617)787-2300	WBZ
New Bedford	(617)997-3349	WBSM
Nebraska		
Omaha	(402)346-6300	WOW
New York		
Albany	(518)462-6445	WROW
Buffalo	(716)885-4357	WYSL
Huntington	(516)423-1400	WGSM
New York City	(212)586-6666	WMCA
Rochester	(716)546-1234	WBBF
Syracuse	(315)474-7441	WHEN
Utica/Rome	(315)797-0120	WTLB
North Carolina		
Raleigh/Durham	(919)832-7578	WRAL-TV
Ohio		
Cincinnati	(513)651-1666	WLW
Cleveland	(216)861-0235	WERE
Youngstown	(216)744-5153	WFMJ
Oklahoma		
Oklahoma City	(405)848-2212	KWTV
Pennsylvania		
Altoona	(814)944-9336	WFBG
Philadelphia	(215)477-5312	WFIL
Pittsburgh	(412)333-9370	KDKA
Rhode Island		
Providence	(401)274-2340	WJAR

If You Are In	Dial This Local Number	Sponsoring Station
Tennessee		
Memphis	(901)278-6316	WDIA
Nashville	(615)227-1478	WVOL
Texas		
Dallas	(214)637-4357	KLIF
Houston	(713)526-3001	KILT
Washington		
Seattle/Tacoma	(206)623-4540	KING
West Virginia		
Charleston	(304)344-8311	WTIP
Wheeling	(304)232-7090	WWVA
Wisconsin		
Milwaukee	(414)342-3036	WISN

6.

National Associations

While a large number of organizations have been set up to study the problems of aging and to lobby on issues important to older people, only a few are membership groups that older people can join both to receive special benefits and to be represented on matters related to the aging process.

NATIONAL COUNCIL OF SENIOR CITIZENS (NCSC)
1511 K Street, N.W., Washington, D.C. 20036

The NSCS, with a membership of over 3 million, was developed by organized labor in the early 1960s to urge the passage of Medicare. It has continued to focus on national issues and legislation relating to aging, and is now moving into the areas of state and local issues as well.

211

The national NCSC office maintains a list of more than three thousand local senior citizens clubs and associations throughout the United States. If you wish to know what groups are active in your area, simply write to the NCSC and ask for the information.

Gold Card membership in the NCSC costs $2.50 a year for members of affiliated clubs and $3 a year for others ($1 additional for a spouse). Members may purchase prescription drugs from NCSC's Direct Drug Service, paying only the actual cost of the drugs and their handling, rather than the "marked-up" price in commercial drug stores. Members who are sixty-five and over may join NCSC's group health insurance plan, which covers the costs of many services that Medicare will not pay for. For those under sixty-five, a special plan is available that converts automatically to the group plan when the member turns sixty-five. In addition, life insurance is available to members up to age eighty-five. No physical examination is required for these insurance policies.

The NCSC Travel Service helps members travel at lower cost than would be possible through commercial travel agencies. It will plan trips, obtain tickets, make reservations, and handle other details for members.

The NCSC's *Senior Citizen News* is sent to members every month. It describes legislation under consideration by Congress and what NCSC is doing to promote the welfare of all older people. It also publishes accounts of activities of local clubs.

AMERICAN ASSOCIATION OF RETIRED PERSONS (AARP)/NATIONAL RETIRED TEACHERS ASSOCIATION

(NRTA) 1909 K Street, N.W., Washington, D.C. 20006

With a combined membership of over 5 million retired educators and other retired white-collar workers and professionals, the AARP/NRTA serves as a lobbying group on any issue directly or indirectly affecting older people. The NRTA was founded in the late 1940s to help teachers who had served their communities improve their lot as retirees. A decade later, the AARP was formed to represent and serve all other retired persons who are concerned about the relative neglect of issues on aging.

Membership in the NRTA is open to anyone who has been employed in any capacity in a school system or has served as a home instructor. Dues are $2 per year. Members receive six issues of the *NRTA Journal*, a monthly news bulletin; prescription drugs delivered to the home at reasonable prices; travel service; eligibility for group health insurance plans; fee-free employment service in some areas; discount privileges in some hotels and motels and with some auto rental firms; and other benefits.

AARP membership ($2 per year) is open to anyone fifty-five years old or older. Benefits of membership are similar to those for NRTA members, with the addition of consumer information, a health education program, educational courses, and a volunteer tax aide program to assist members in filing income tax forms.

NATIONAL ASSOCIATION OF RETIRED FEDERAL EMPLOYEES (NARFE)
1909 Q Street, N.W., Washington, D.C. 20009

NARFE's membership of over 180,000 is largely concentrated in the Washington area, California and Florida. For $4 per year, members receive a monthly magazine, *Retirement Life*; pamphlets on the legal aspects of retirement planning; a prescription drug service; and health, life, and auto insurance. Membership is open to all retired federal employees; federal employees who have chosen not to retire yet, although they have met the minimum requirements for retirement; and their spouses and survivors.

SENIOR ADVOCATES INTERNATIONAL
1825 K Street, N.W., Washington, D.C. 20006
Senior Advocates International acts as an advocate and spokesman for people over fifty. It seeks to bring about changes in business and government, particularly in the areas of pensions, age discrimination in employment, health insurance, credit, and public services. For a $5 fee, members can obtain group insurance, vitamins and prescription drugs, rental cars, photo service, and travel service at lower than commercial prices. Members also receive *Senior Advocate* magazine monthly.

In addition to the membership organizations, one group serves as a technical consultant to groups wishing to organize and to organizations concerned with solving the problems of older people. *The National Council on the Aging* (1828 L Street, N.W., Washington, D.C. 20006) can provide pamphlets, books, and technical advice and will refer people to organizations that can assist them with their problems. Write to the NCOA for a pamphlet listing current publications.